SUPPORTING ARSENAL
IS A FUNNY OLD GAME
SERIOUSLY FUNNY, YET FUNNILY SERIOUS

Published by
Legends Publishing

E-mail david@legendspublishing.net
Website www.legendspublishing.net

Copyright 2016

ISBN: 978-1-906796-58-7

Cover artwork by Jamie Fulker

For more information:
@jfdoodles or http://jfdoodles.com

CONTENTS

INTRODUCTION

somehow doubt there is any sport anywhere in the world that has more clichés associated with it than football, most particularly in the United Kingdom. I could be completely wrong, not being a linguist, but why do players, managers and commentators have such a rich heritage in churning out the same well used, often meaningless (outside of Football) lines with such regularity as they do on our shores?

So, whether I am over the moon, sick as a parrot, tired from running my socks off, concerned about a wet Wednesday night in Bolton, or just anxious I may lose the dressing room, there is nobody I would rather talk to than a fellow supporter who understands me – because chatting about football is therapeutic – and a pastime that all like-minded fans enjoy.

For me, and in reality, for most of us, we think we can manage the team, select the best eleven and formulate the appropriate tactics. Well, we can, can't we? We all chat about it in the pub, or the café, prior to a match – then with our pals long after the final whistle has blown. When I started writing about Arsenal, or should I say 'blogging' about my beloved Gunners, all I was doing was jotting down pretty much what I had discussed, or told my long-suffering mates, over a pint. It is why my pieces often have a conversational style to them, and I like to think, or at least hope, that is why fellow fans enjoy them.

The second constant theme in all our football following lives is humour, and if we are honest, at times, that humour can be black. I would go as far as to say that, as a fan, if you can't laugh at your own team, and at yourself on occasion, you need to do some soul searching and remind yourself that it is, after all, a hobby that you should derive pleasure from. Basically, at the end of the day, Brian, when all is said and done, and the fat lady is singing, the Legend that is Jimmy Greaves had it pretty spot on when he used to say that 'Football is a Funny Old Game!'

It struck me that perhaps the perfect way to combine our enjoyment of hearing other fans' stories, with an essential comedic element, would be to approach some chaps who could assist me with both. As most people will acknowledge, Arsenal is a glamourous club and a global brand that has always attracted the rich and famous – from British Royalty to Pop royalty... from Olympians to Hollywood stars. However, there is one species of celebrity that Arsenal has lured a bizarrely high proportion of supporters from down the years – comedians. So welcome to 'Supporting Arsenal is a Funny Old Game.'

So, join me on what I sincerely hope is an entertaining and hilarious exploration of the journey into Goonerdom, and beyond, for sixteen fans who just happen to have made a career out of making people laugh. And what a collection I have assembled in this book – many are already household names – with several falling into the 'national treasure' category.

At the same time, though, I found that, like all fans, they are very serious about their football. Hence this book's sub title – 'Seriously funny, yet funnily serious.' Because you have to learn early-doors that, no matter how developed your sense of humour, surviving as an Arsenal supporter is a serious business!

Well, all that remains for me to says is; both I and all my collaborators on this book have most certainly gone the extra mile, and given 110% to ensure the quality of our end product... We hope you enjoy the book!

Dave Seager

FOREWORD

When I go to the Emirates these days I feel proud of the diverse crowd we attract – actors, TV presenters and radio hosts as well as all the stand-up comedians. Every now and then I even meet the occasional person who isn't a performer or in the media. I'm joking of course. In fact even the Platinum members I'm surrounded by in the elite confines of Club Level, where I sit, are mostly thoroughly normal people who save up all their disposable funds so they can afford to watch Arsenal every other week. But it does feel like we have more than our fair share of celebrities and, especially, professional funny people supporting our great club. Obviously, we are a tad poncey and showbiz as an institution, which is possibly one reason why we attract a good number of celebrity fans. There's also the geographical fact of being based in the bit of north London which is much nicer than the other lot's bit of north London down the road. Let's face it: we're a smart, cultured, civilised bunch. Well, mostly. Occasionally, fights do break out among our own fans, but every team has its lunatic fringe element, right?

Actually, it does seem like particularly good timing on Dave Seager's part to gather this impressive gaggle of Arsenal-supporting comedy types to celebrate their support for the weirdly hilarious sporting and cultural entity that is Arsenal Football Club right now. Being any kind of football supporter is a darkly comic experience for much of the time, but I reckon being an Arsenal fan at this particular moment in history is especially rich with farcical potential. We're the only club for whom finishing in the top four every year for decades is both "a trophy" and a reason for apathy and boredom. And of course the cause of those fisticuffs which happen every now and then among our supporters is that we have a uniquely divided fan-base with actual acronyms assigned to the tribes who define themselves by their view of our current manager - the "AKBs" (Arsene Knows Best) and the "WOBs" (Wenger Out Brigade). Everybody who supports Arsenal has to have a view on Le Boss. It seems like there are very few Arsenal fans who just shrug and think, 'Yeah, he's doing fine'. Who knows, maybe by the time this book comes out we'll all have calmed down, but I somehow doubt it. We are, I am almost proud to say, a bit of a laughing stock among other fans who regards us either as perennially spoiled glory-hunters who should be happy with our relentless Champions League adventures which always end in disappointment, or else delusional fools clinging on to past glories. But maybe this unique situation with our manager, and the very strong opinions he inspires, is the reason we also seem to have way more blogs, Fan TV channels, YouTubers, dedicated Arsenal tweeters and podcasts, as well as famous fans, than any normal club.

Here I must declare that I co-host my own Arsenal podcast clumsily called *Footballistically Arsenal*, named after a famous Wenger coinage ("Theo Walcott has improved footballistically"). And many of our recurring guests happen to grace the pages of this fine tome. Indeed, one of my favourite regulars, Alex Brooker, helped inspire Dave to write this book, having got to know one another as seat neighbours at the Emirates. For me, Brooker is the dream celebrity fan. He's famous because he's talented - funny, clever and deeply likeable, and he's also entirely free of bullshit. Everything he says about Arsenal, both in his chapter in this book and on his appearances on our podcast, is genuine. He's a real fan first, but he happens to be brilliantly funny about it.

I think that's true of all the supporters gathered in these pages. From legends like Matt Lucas and his good friend, the comedic actor Paul Kaye, to the young and thrusting stand-up, writer and thespian Tom Rosenthal, who is also a trusted *Footballistically Arsenal* regular – none of these people became fans because it felt somehow trendy to do so after reading Nick Hornby's *Fever Pitch*, which is what I sometimes think supporters of other clubs assume about our celeb-filled fanbase. They're all lifelong Arsenal fans. It's just that they're funnier about it than the rest of us. Enjoy their insights and memories and jokes, and well done to Dave Seager for bringing them all together in this endlessly entertaining volume.

Boyd Hilton Editor of Heat Magazine

IAN STONE STONE STONE

t is impossible not to like Ian Stone, but trust me, it is entirely possible, as a passionate football fan, to be a tiny bit jealous of him. Not because he has been making audiences laugh, pretty much weekly, at the Comedy Store for over 20 years. Not because he was voted in the Top 10 UK Stand-ups by *The Independent*. Not even because his particular brand of observational humour and storytelling has taken him all over the world – to comedy festivals and to entertain our troops. I couldn't do what he does anyway, but because of all the above, until recently his work allowed him to chat football with his comedy chums on BT Sport's *The Football's On* – which he hosted. Not only that, but he was able to chat *more* football on the post-match *Rock 'n' Roll Football* show on Absolute Radio, co-hosting with Arsenal Legend Ian Wright. A gig he has passed on to Robb Beckett this season. As if that was not enough, in his spare time, he dissects the goings-on at his beloved Arsenal with his pals on the most famous Arsenal Podcast: *The Tuesday Club*, (more of which later).

WHERE IT BEGAN

Ian grew up in a North London Jewish household in the 1960's and his football education came primarily from his father. Now, whilst his dad was undoubtedly an Arsenal fan, he did what would be unheard of today (but was not unusual back then), and went to Highbury one week and White Hart Lane the next. In the Tottenham Double-Winning Season (yes, the last time they won the league), Ian's dad went to every Spurs home game whilst doing the same at Arsenal. Stone hastens to add that his support was never confused – he was never taken to Tottenham; only to Arsenal. He first went as a seven-year-old in the 1969/70 season, a season in which Arsenal were to end a 17-year

photo courtesy of Stuart Macfarlane and Arsenal FC

trophy drought. The first trip was enough, though. The atmosphere; the red shirt; a young boy just knew: *"I want to be here, this is where I want to be, and that was it."*

He went to matches with his dad for many years as a boy, and they would always stand right in the middle of the North Bank where Stone fondly recalls that the reality was he could barely see. *"What I remember is a lot of the play in the middle of the field and goals at the Clock End, but everything that came into the penalty area I had no chance. Everyone would go up and I would think, 'What's going on, then!' and once in a while you would hear a roar and you knew Arsenal had scored. And then what would happen is you would fall down about 20 steps until you hit a crash barrier. That's what I remember: really just loving the atmosphere."*

The father and son pilgrimage continued, and by the mid-1970s it was to every game, all through the bleak later-Bertie Mee era. *"I remember being with my dad in the terrible years: '73... '74... years when we ended up finishing 17th or something. We had Terry Mancini playing for us – a lot of terrible players. I went to ALL those games. You know – those games with tiny attendances? Standing there with my dad, thinking 'What am I doing here? What are we watching this rubbish for..?"*

In truth, however, NOT being there was never a consideration; and even in those dark times there was one shiny beacon of hope that had arrived in the form of a stick of a teenage lad from Ireland at the end of the 1971 Double season. Yes, Liam Brady – as for so many Gunners of a certain age – was the first Arsenal hero for Stone.

"In terms of heroes, Brady was the first one for me. Charlie George was slightly before my time really, although I did start going quite regularly in 1972. Through the mid-70s it wasn't much of a team. Brady turned up and you just went 'WOW!' My son is 13 now and is left-footed and – while he is obviously not the player that Brady was – there are times he just has his body shaped in the same way, and it transports me instantly back in time to watching Liam Brady. He was the 'One'. I had just never seen a player so comfortable on the ball really – not playing for us, anyway. There were certain players I liked in that team, but he was always the one for me."

A JEWISH 80S HOOLIGAN: FUNNY OR NOT FUNNY?

The catalyst for Stone to begin following Arsenal without his dad was, sadly, his parents divorcing. He fell in with a crowd at Highbury and was soon going to as many Away as Home matches. His peers, however, were not from his community or school. The Jewish Free School in Camden, where he has since described himself as the only funny guy among 1,500 Jews was, at the time, reflective of some of the ills of late '70s and early '80s society, and most certainly early '80s football. Stone describes regular run-ins with the students of Holloway Boys School, (which Charlie George had attended a few years earlier); they would arrive in droves and stand outside the Jewish Free School, waiting for the Jewish kids to leave, whilst doing mock Nazi salutes in unison. Shockingly, genuine anti-Semitism was very de rigueur back then, which leads to the obvious question of how he squared this with the terrace sentiment and songs that were the norm at Highbury at the time - whether his beloved Gunners were playing Tottenham or not.

"It was horrible and obviously I wasn't singing it, but of course I was with people that were. I was not a particularly devout Jew, but I went to the synagogue every week. So, on a Saturday, I would go the synagogue in the morning and to the game in the afternoon. It was incredibly strange to be transported from the synagogue, where you are standing there doing all this chanting and singing about how the Jewish God is great – then to be amongst thousands going on about gassing Jews

only four hours later. Standing with these guys, who are after all are supposed to be on your side. It's a very weird juxta-position."

In many ways the '80s was a low point. Not just at Arsenal – it was all of football. If you wanted to follow your team you sort of had to accept it; and, if we are being honest, even *embrace* it to some degree. Stone describes his love of following the national team – always at Wembley, and on occasion abroad – but at its worst, the hard core of the English support seemed to be a collection of the worst elements of the hooligans from all the clubs. It reached a point where he loved watching the national team play, but almost wanted them to lose, just to make the fans unhappy. Fortunately this disconnect was to change after *Italia '90*.

"Football in the '80s was hateful in many ways. You would go away and hear monkey chants, particularly up North. I remember going to away games and there was a lot of violence, plenty of fighting. Lots of running away as I recall, and I was knocked down by a police horse in Bristol! To be honest I am disgusted with my mother for letting me go. From 15 onwards I was going to Away games in places like Derby, Bristol and Stoke, and it was dangerous, and we were going on horrible football specials with drunken grown men."

Given how much humour we all see in football, perhaps then was a rich source of material for a stand-up comedian. Strangely the answer lies in the changing face of football in the eyes of the nation, and the cross-section of society that now follows the national game. The reality is that football now features heavily in Stone's repertoire, but whilst, ironically, the jokes arrive courtesy of the low points at that time and early in his career, perhaps for the first ten years, even the mention of the word 'football' could switch off an audience.

"Most of the women were just not interested, for a start. You have to remember that back then, the 'alternative comedy' circuit was incredibly 'right on' and it was a reaction against all that old-school stuff and football felt – at that time – like part of that."

Football back then, Stone suggests, was almost like a dirty little secret. As he says: if you think about the violence, Hillsborough, Thatcher, and how her government felt about football and hooliganism, it reflected the views of much of middle class society. Football was violent and dirty, and there was nothing pleasant about it, except for the game itself of course.

"The game was the thing you went for and you loved the game, but it was dangerous. Looking back, I put myself in so many perilous situations; but it was normal to get on these trains, to go to these towns

and get shit thrown at you. I got chased three miles back to Lime Street station. I got the last train back from Cardiff and was so lucky not to get beaten up. I got beaten up in Wolverhampton and there were so many occasions where it could have got a lot worse. You just have to remember that people died at football then; people were stabbed. We took risks to go and see the game we love, to see The Arsenal and I can't believe we did – but there it is."

Now, of course, football has changed completely, and for the main part, it is safe, sanitised even; but just sometimes you have the odd occasion that takes you back to the good/bad old days and for Stone the Capital Cup North London Derby at the Lane in 2015 was one of those instances. He describes it as the most brilliant and the most dangerous thing he had done in years. Having parked a fair way from the ground he rode the bus right to the ground, but it was unnerving as soon as he stepped off.

"I mean, I'm vaguely recognisable as an Arsenal fan – so I'm walking down to White Hart Lane and I'm getting the '...there he is – that Arsenal Wanker' (and far worse), and I thought I should have worn a hat or something, as with this nose and glasses I'm fairly obvious. So I took my glasses off but now I couldn't see. It was so, so ridiculous."

Then, whilst waiting outside the Away End for his mate, Stone started chatting to another Gunner, who seemed a pleasant middle-aged chap, but who then proceeded to pick up a bottle and throw it at the passing Tottenham throng. "I said 'Don't do that!' – obviously not wanting to appear associated with this guy; but too late. A copper comes over and just looks at the guys and me and starts laughing and just says 'Stop it, you!' That's all. I guess he knows there will be bigger fish to fry than a semi-well-known Arsenal comic and his idiot companion, as the helicopters buzz overhead."

Already beginning to feel like he is in a time warp back to the '80s, he rings his mate Rich – who has the tickets – to see where he is, and the response is: 'I am on the train, I am nearly there... Oh, sorry! Got to go – it's kicking off!" Stone recalls thinking, 'We are two middle aged men with kids, and we are both putting ourselves in situations!'

When he was finally safely in the Away End, Stone described the atmosphere as 'amazing, properly hateful, but hateful in a good way'. "It is crackling; you know what it is like. I do think the atmosphere in White Hart Lane is fantastic. For a North London Derby night game you can't beat it – but I would certainly not be taking my 13 year old along. No way."

photo courtesy of Stuart Macfarlane and Arsenal FC

The Arsenal travelling support were kept in the ground for half an hour afterwards, and when they finally get out there is tear gas, there's riot police and there are 5,000 or so Tottenham fans who have waited for us for 40 minutes. The obvious thought is 'Haven't these guys got homes to go to?'

"The police want to walk us all the way down Seven Sisters Road, but I am parked elsewhere. So I say to a copper, 'Listen – can I go through the housing estate?' And he looks at me like 'REALLY? At 10.30 at night?' I said 'Trust me – it is safer to walk through a housing estate at night than down Tottenham High Road with Tottenham fans on either side shouting abuse!' I got to my car at 10.45 and I let out a huge sigh of relief. Like fucking hell, I've made it. I am going to be alright!"

That night got him thinking about the football scene of his youth. That night Flamini had scored twice to beat the old enemy, and everything about it felt like a throwback to the '80s. It made him realize that what he missed from that period was the atmosphere in the ground – not the violence and the danger. But when ventured the observation that surely *nobody* would miss the violence, Stone is not so sure – because so many of the guys waiting for the Arsenal fans that night were in their 50s and, as he says, may have kids or even grandkids, which beggars belief.

"I see this behaviour and I think 'My God!' But it does make for a great atmosphere as these guys know what it can be like – so I guess I am torn. I miss some of that, because it truly crackled that night. Obviously Flamini netting a 25-yard volley ten minutes from the end helped. That's a nice moment, right? And obviously we enjoy it; but there were bad things going on back then, and I am glad that those times are over."

Getting back to the anti-Semitism and racism of that time, Stone does feel that – in the main – it has disappeared from the game and from the stadium. He suggests that, to a large degree, fans in football grounds have become self-policing. People have thankfully realised over time that those songs and chants were disgusting. There really are not that many seriously anti-Semitic people out there. There are some proper racists of course, but they have been marginalised – particularly at Arsenal. At West Ham, and to a degree Chelsea, there is still a racist element – but not at Arsenal, not really. There's a little bit at the odd Away game but even still, it feels slightly embarrassing (from Stone's perspective).

FOOTBALL AND HOOLIGANISM DEFINITELY FUNNY

All this brings us conveniently back to the fact that football, now, is more of an acceptable subject for his own writing and material. Not only does football have wider appeal 30 years on, but it is the very things that made it a taboo subject back then that provide the rich comedy gold today. In reality – making light of the horrible times, and reliving the mixture of fear and adrenaline is bloody funny in the hands of an expert observational comedian like Stone.

"I have written more stuff about being a football fan in the last six months than I have ever done. It's just: one – I am more involved in that world, and two – there is so much funny stuff that goes on, and I feel now I am able to share it with people."

At the heart of Stone's witty trip down memory lane is a section where he talks about himself as an Arsenal hooligan of that time. Of course, the truth is that Ian was *not* a hooligan and was undoubtedly a bit of a coward – so his act describes himself being with people who would be punching people and shouting *"Go on – punch him!"* from ten yards behind – then, *'Go on – I am with you!"* I am sure you can visualise Stone acting this out at the Comedy Store and laughing at the self-ridicule and humour?

Well, I'm sure *most* of us would be laughing – and in the main, Stone has had huge success with this routine. Until Christmas 2015, when one member of the audience was *"an utterly proper old school, big, fat, tattooed 50-year-old Millwall racist."* This particular genuine hooligan failed to see the funny side of Stone's 'pretend to be a hooligan' stories and he was heckling continuously. He began by accusing Stone of not being a real hooligan, which was hardly a surprise to everyone else in the audience. He then proceeded to try and tell Stone how he and his Millwall crew tried to steal the clock from Highbury. He did not take kindly to Stone's quite reasonable observation that they must have had *"bloody big screwdrivers and a helicopter"* and was getting angrier and angrier before coming out with what he thought was a classic heckle. *"Hang on a minute, mate!"* he goes, in front of everyone. *"You're an Arsenal fan but you're Jewish. How does that work, then? That doesn't work!"* To which Stone responded instantly: "*Whereas being a prick and a Millwall fan works perfectly*!" At which point our friend from South East London tried to attack Stone on stage – which was the end of the gig!

Despite the slight concern that these guys are still out there, Stone is continuing to make his audiences laugh by laughing at himself, and at what he (and so many of us) did in the Eighties. He always gets a few boos and some stick at the outset – because he is a Gooner – which is fine and expected, but then he tells stories which are intrinsically funny: such as waving a ten pound note in front of a Northerner saying, *"There you go! Buy yourself a house, you Northern Bastards!"* In his routine he says, *"I used to do this in the Eighties, but I would have to borrow a ten pound note from my mum every week. She would say 'I can't afford to lend you a tenner, Ian!' to which I would say, 'Don't worry – I'll bring it back. I just want to highlight the economic disparity, Mum!"*

It's hysterical now when he tells it, and of course he tells his audiences he is not proud of it, but the truth is: he is a little bit proud of it. That is the material he rather enjoys; but Stone is acutely aware of lines he won't cross. For example: *'Always a victim and it's never your fault'* should never be sung. We all know what happened at Hillsborough should never be a subject for humour; for Stone and, I hope, all *true* football fans. So, in summary: the football material mixes well with the rest of his routine; so much so, that Stone is considering writing a whole show based on football aimed at you guys – so watch this space.

TV AND RADIO BANTER

In discussing his television work we touched on the 'Mock the Week'-style panel programmes that are so in vogue – and he of course has appeared on many of them – but it is the football chat equivalent of the genre that has grown in popularity simultaneously.

"I can't get on Mock the Week *anymore. Look at this face: it's 25 years too old for TV, most of the time. But Sports TV – they give me my own show, and I'll sit with good comics, we'll talk about football and it's funny. It's great because people like that sort of stuff. I mean Fantasy Football all those years ago maybe started it."*

Stone (as you might expect) is spot on; and it probably did begin – at least on our screens – with Baddiel (his primary school pal) and Skinner's *Fantasy Football League* in 1994. On radio, one could argue it began with Danny Baker's *606*. Amazingly, the former only ran for two years and three series; but – like the game that inspired the concept – that show gave birth to a myriad of television and radio shows, and they are as popular now as they ever were, perhaps more so. *talk-SPORT* – love it or hate it – has been on the air since 1995, and in its present, predominantly sports chat format, since 1998.

In recent times, the concept of a group of individuals talking football has been given a further iteration by the rise of the podcast, and Stone (not surprisingly) features heavily across a world that combines his two loves: football and comedy. It is why he believes his BT Sports show worked was popular, and why so many Arsenal fans love the *Tuesday Club* podcast.

"Bottom line is that football fans love talking about football and the associated humour; and they love listening to others talking about football. This is why The Tuesday Club *works so well, I think, and it is what the TV show tries to do as well. The pod is people who have known each other a long time, talking about something they love."*

All of the 'Tuesday Club' regulars – Stone, Alan Davies, Keith Dover, DJ Tayo and Damian Harris – sit together at the Emirates.

Stone also has the honour of being a regular columnist in the Arsenal Magazine – a gig he inherited from another Arsenal funny-man/actor – Paul Kaye. Andy Exley at the Club was obviously aware of the podcast, and when Kay called it a day after six years, Stone was delighted to receive the call. Being Arsenal, I am sure the global circulation both in hard copy and online is colossal – but Stone is typically low-key and modest on the subject.

"I think it gets read a lot in Indonesia. I write once a month, and it is a nice thing to be part of the Club for a fan. I got taken for a little tour of the ground when I started and that was all very nice. I get to express an opinion."

Of course, given that it is an *Arsenal* publication – it might be fair to say that the opinion expressed is not always as frank as the one he might express on the pod – or on his TV or radio shows, perhaps?

WENGER AND FOOTBALL HEROES

Getting back to the football: Stone admits that – with work and other commitments – he was unable to be a regular at Highbury in the late 1980s and early '90s. Whilst obviously still a Gunner at heart he was not a regular for much of the Graham era. He only returned full-time in 1995. Although the timing was coincidental – as Stone says, *"I got back into it in about '95 and then Arséne Wenger turned up and I enjoyed watching the emergence of a great team."*

Just before the little-known Frenchman arrived at Arsenal, there was a moment that heralded the new dawn: *"When Patrick Vieira came on against Sheffield Wednesday it was astonishing. It was one of only three or four moments I remember everybody just going: 'What the hell?' £4.5m (or whatever it was) and he just ran the game. He was just 20 and we all thought, "Where has he been?"*

Stone admits that most of his greatest Arsenal moments have come post-Wenger, and – not surprisingly – when asked about favourite players, the majority (barring the aforementioned Brady) have figured, or evolved, in Wenger teams.

"Dennis Bergkamp, I knew about him: we'd all seen him play – and then suddenly you are watching him in the flesh and thinking he is every bit as good as we imagined. Anelka just showing up as a kid and being brilliant; and Petit and Vieira together – I loved those two. And of course, Overmars: fast and naturally right-footed yet unbelievable playing on the left."

"Pires, just genius, utter genius. And Henry, who was like nothing I had ever seen. I still think Bergkamp is the best player ever to play for Arsenal, but Henry, I've never seen anyone like him. My other son (who is 17 now) is not into football at all, he is a ballet dancer... well he is a dancer. But he loves watching ballet, and not football – but he loved watching Henry because he can appreciate the aesthetic beauty, and the grace in his movement, and what he did."

A special mention too for Ian Wright, whom Stone describes as the most natural finisher he has even seen play. . *"Every time he was through on goal you're thinking 'goal'. Or at least you knew he was going to hit the target and work the keeper."*

It must be wonderful now to have worked with one of his heroes?

For Stone it is no longer so strange, as 'Wrighty' has become a mate; although – having said that – having a hero as a mate is still a bit weird. *"One time he phoned, I answered and he's singing down the line 'Ian Stone Stone Stone' I said you can't do that, Wrighty – it's just too weird for me. You are weirding me out in all sorts of ways!"*

MATCHES, MOMENTS AND FANS

Discussing matches with Stone is particularly interesting because he observes, quite shrewdly, that it is often little *moments* in matches that you recall vividly or fondly. The obvious example that comes to mind is the 1979 FA Cup Final – which he went to with his dad – and which is often described as one of the greatest Finals. The truth of course is that it was a dull game with an exciting and crazy five minutes tagged on the end, culminating in *the* moment – Brady... to Rix... to Sunderland... and the resulting mayhem.

In the recent past Stone describes the FA Cup Quarter Final win at old Trafford in March 2015 as unequivocally one of the best nights of his life. There were over 9,000 of us that made that Monday evening trip, and in the season reviews and on social media, the players all acknowledged the contribution of the fans in the win. Just being in there that night was so special: singing *"49, 49 undefeated..."* on repeat, and watching their fans leave early after Welbeck scored. It felt, to Stone and to everyone who was there, as if we were sucking the ball into the net.

In about a dozen visits to Old Trafford over 30-odd years, Stone had never seen the team win there, or even draw. All the way back to the '70s when he went there and we lost 2-0 and Gordon McQueen scored two headers.

The thing that's funny about that was they kept us in for 30 minutes after the game and then Gerald Sinstadt (BBC) came on to the pitch to interview Gordon McQueen – the Man of the Match – and there's only us Gunners left in the ground! We all started singing instantly *"We all agree... Gordon McQueen is a wanker!"* and they had to go off and wait for us to leave.

After the game Stone had accepted an offer from Wrighty to take him and his son back in his BBC car as he was there for '*Match of the Day*', this became a funny story in itself. He approached the BBC compound only to be stopped by a surly and burly steward barring his way – and whilst it still sounded odd saying it, Stone said something along the lines of *"I need to go in there. I am a mate of Wrighty's and he is giving us a lift home.*

"The steward said, 'Wait there,' looking at me very sternly and I just take a step forward – nothing more than that – and he shoves me in the chest, "Wait there!" but as he has done it, Wrighty has popped his head out of the cabin and shouted 'Stoney, Stoney! Over here...' So with a big grin on my face and a sarcastic tone in my voice I said, 'Excuse me. I am going to see my mate now' and we just walked past him just thinking 'Nice one, Wrighty, that was perfect timing. I could have paid you for that.'" Then we were whisked out of Old Trafford in a BBC S Class Merc. What a night!

Being in a privileged position on television and radio has afforded Stone opportunities most fans can only dream of; interviewing Thierry Henry was one such occasion, and it brings us to another favourite 'moment' and, indeed, match.

Ian is friends with Amy Lawrence (who wrote the superb '*Invincible*' book), and he mentioned their mutual friendship with Thierry, and how she had described the Leeds FA Cup match – when Henry returned – as an 'out-of-body experience'. Stone relates to that, but he described it to Henry as akin to a Springsteen concert;

"That's what he it felt like to me – because the whole night was like a warm-up, and the crowd were just waiting for the main event. Henry started laughing and got quite emotional. He said he was a fan at that point, and had come back as a fan, so to come on and do what he did, to score such a beautiful Henry goal..."

"There was something crazy and I think it was something different to anything I had experienced at football. He told me he sat in the dressing room until about one in the morning because he couldn't really believe what he had done and what had transpired. He didn't get changed, he didn't want to go, or for the moment to be over. That's a fan talking – that's not a player."

For Stone (and for all of us, I suspect) it was a mad, one-off night. Someone told him that they were on the Holloway Road that night, and when Arsenal scored they had never heard anything like it – and he had lived around there all his life.

Looking back at treasured Highbury memories, strangely – given all the players Stone discussed earlier were offensive – both feature good old English centre backs. The first Highbury afternoon that came to his mind was the match against Everton that secured the league title. Stone remembers it as *"A glorious afternoon, a glorious, stupid afternoon. Bloody hell, Arsenal! It has changed down here when Bould plays a perfect ball forward and Adams chests it down and expertly volleys it in the bottom corner and stands there as if to say 'What?' It was amazing and we all just start laughing. I remember looking around at 38,000 people laughing because we could not believe what we were watching. Unbelievable football, and the way we were playing, we swatted Everton aside and won the title."*

One of his all-time favourite games involves Arsenal warrior Martin Keown, when he scored two in the last five minutes to win the game against Shakhtar Donetsk. The importance of the match to the club cannot be understated back at Highbury after two unsuccessful Champions League campaigns at Wembley. The Gunners however, went 2-0 down in the first 30 minutes but pulled one back just on half time. They were still losing 2-1 with five to go and Keown – the unlikely hero – pops up and scores twice in five minutes to win the game. Martin's face was a picture and you could just see what it meant to him.

"So I went home and my partner asks 'How did you get on?' 'We did it. We won it!' I tell her, 'It was all about the fans.' Of course she looked at me with genuine pity, but about half an hour later I watched the highlights and Keown was interviewed. He was there still – wide eyes – saying 'it's the fans, it's all about the fans: they did it for us.' I turned to her and said 'See? See? I told you we did that."

As he reaffirms, it is one of those occasions – like United away in the FA Cup in *2015* – *"where as fans you have that connection with the players and they feel it, you know they do. When they talk about it in the match programme, or on the website afterwards, you think 'Yes! I am not just imagining this.'"*

Another personal favourite memory for Stone also features Keown: a defining moment in his last season for the club, when we drew 0-0 away with Manchester United during the Undefeated Season. Stone was not at Old Trafford, as he was in South Africa doing a comedy festival. He was watching the game in a bar, surrounded by South African Man United fans, all wearing the shirts. Whilst not wearing colours himself, he felt it soon became fairly obvious where his allegiances lay. Arsenal weren't playing that well, and it was a tough old game; when van Nistlerooy got Paddy sent off the atmosphere in the room became a tad difficult for him.

"I did not want to be shouting and screaming too much, but I was so pissed off with him for basically cheating to get our skipper sent off. So when he missed that penalty, honestly this is how it felt to me. I was aware of this roar in the room and I realised that it was me as everyone turned to look at me with angry faces. You know - that sort of primal shout that involuntarily comes out of you."

Stone has subsequently met Martin Keown and told him that his reaction to van Nistlerooy is one of his favourite moments as an Arsenal supporter. Keown was slightly embarrassed at the time as a player, but in retirement – as time moves on – he knows that moment, and the togetherness of the team, created a bond with each other and with the fans that saw them through that season. It's that mentality – suggests Stone – which Adams talked about: when he said 'You need at least seven in the trenches with you...' That day you could see the whole team, with Lauren and Parlour, were all up for it.

There have been so many savoured matches and moments at the Emirates and, of course, Wembley. Stone describes the Villa Final as a 'lovely day', but the Newcastle final in 1998 – on the back of the Premiership title being secured – has a special place in his heart. He had a Marc Overmars to score and a two-nil win double bet that won him £120. Alan (Davies) had hired them a limousine. So Ian, Keith, Simon Clayton, their mate, and Alan travelled from Islington to Wembley in style. Of course The Gunners did indeed win 2-0, it was a fabulous match and Wenger's first League and FA Cup Double was secured in fitting style. *"We come out and think 'How shall we get home? Oh, hang on, there's a limo waiting for us...' so we jump in the car to get back; and my son was born the day after – so: a perfect never to be forgotten weekend."*

Sometimes – Stone stresses – it is hard to remember back to individual great days at Highbury, although of course there were so many. It's an age thing, Stoney! Many of the games that come to the fore are more recent. The Barcelona 2-1 was an epic for us all...

"I recall being in the pub afterwards and Jack Whitehall coming in and looking like a four-year-old with his eyes wide, and I remember thinking 'I bet we all look like that' because we had witnessed something special. To play that brilliant team, match them, and ultimately beat them was incredible."

There have been so many moments at the Emirates that he lists: the Arshavin goal from the Barca night; beating Chelsea 3-1 when Walcott scored the third; beating Spurs 5-2 twice... *"But we need to see the team win some trophies there now. That will be the next level up."*

Even games like when we beat Newcastle 1-0 in the 95th minute – with Vermaelen scoring the winner. *"That was pretty spectacular and Van Perise, who I am not a fan of now, that night taunting Tim Krul who had been wasting time for the entire game. Van Persie then going up as if to say 'Go on, mate... Are you still taking your time now? Or are you going to hurry up now, are you?' Krul getting really pissed off with him and [me] thinking 'How brilliant!'"*

It was thoroughly enjoyable chatting to Ian Stone about our mutual love, but there is one thing that came through loud and clear: that for him it is so often not the games that mean so much, but the moments that make those games. It is the funny memories, the individual brilliance, the great goals, and unlikely heroes, passion spilling over from players to team-mates, and of course from players to fans. It is the moments that turn games that make the memories and that forge the connection between those on the pitch and those in the stands.

"Those are the things I remember. It's why you go, right? Those moments..."

ALAN ALAN ALAN DAVIES

Alan Davies, I would guess, is one of the most instantly recognisable faces on British television and, as such, he must be one of Arsenal's most famous fans. I don't have to guess whether he is one of our funniest and, TV aside, any fans who are regular listeners to the most renowned Arsenal Podcast, The Tuesday Club, which he co-hosts with Ian Stone, DJ Tayo, Keith Dover and Damien Harris, will need no convincing.

Davies had been one of the UK's finest stand-ups since graduating from Kent University in 1988, but perhaps became best known to the wider population as the star, in the title role of David Renwick's *Jonathan Creek*. He still returns to the role in one-off specials but at its peak (in 1999), his performances as the mystery solving magician's trick designer, were pulling in over 11 million viewers. In 1998 he was nominated for a BAFTA in the 'Most Popular Actor' category. He did not win, but trust me when I say Wenger's Arsenal bringing home the League and FA Cup Double were far more important to him.

He has also been on our screens for 13 years as the only ever-present panellist on the (until recently) Stephen Fry hosted, QI. Davies has appeared on every single QI ever recorded, and for the whole of all the episodes bar one. That one show he 'missed' (and was only in because he did a pre-recorded scene) was filmed on the 17 May 2006 – a day Davies had a more important engagement at the Stade de France in Paris!

A TALE OF TWO BROTHERS AND A SHIRT

So, where did the Arsenal journey begin for Davies? Well, amazingly and amusingly, it began in a staunch Tottenham household in Loughton, Essex in 1971. Davies' father was Spurs through and through and his elder brother had followed the family tradition, but ironically it is the annoying older brother we have to thank for Alan's betrayal. Aged five, Davies was already massively into his football and regularly played with his brother in the back garden. As you would expect with a two-year age difference there was already sibling rivalry. His brother was the proud owner of the lilywhite Tottenham shirt with the navy cockerel on the chest. It was a lovely shirt and hard not to admire, but the younger Davies, whilst wanting his own football shirt, did not want the same one as his irritating older brother. His brother felt the same so, inadvertently, offered some advice that would change the course of Davies's life *"Why don't you get an Arsenal one they are top of the league?"* As Davies said; *"Of course he has no idea at that age what he was saying – he knew not what he had done!"*

He is not certain why his mum, when taking him to the sports shop to buy his shirt, did not say anything, knowing her husband's strong allegiance to the other side of North London. He will never know as she tragically passed away, losing a battle with leukaemia just a year later. She showed him the beautiful red shirt with the white sleeves and there was no going back. Davies loved it and the purchase was made.

"She asked whether I would like the number nine on the back. 'That is John Radford who scores all the goals' she told me. I said no I want to be the captain so she sewed Frank McLintock's number five on the back and the Cannon on the chest. I have still got the shirt somewhere, although the number has fallen off."

Davies describes the episode in his own wonderful 2009 book *My Favourite People and Me* 1978 to 1988. He could have, and had it not been sibling rivalry, should have been a Spurs fan. The moment where his life could have taken a tragic turn:

"There is no single moment that could have gone as badly wrong as the moment in 1971, when I chose Arsenal. What a terrifyingly close near slip into a pit of bitterness and despair, of false dawns and continual second best disappointment. To have never had the joys of Arsenal heroes like Liam Brady and David Rocastle...That was the Great Escape of mythological proportions, a turn-to-stone, don't-look-back-or-someone's-a-pillar-of-salt moment. For Spurs are truly shamefully terrible and Arsenal are the custodians of human decency in a world of lies."

To be fair to Alan's dad, in the face of his youngest son's rebellion, he did take his lad to his first match against Stoke at the start of the following season. He clearly remembers being carried into Highbury on

his father's shoulders, and although his newly adopted team, reigning champions, lost by a goal to nil, he was smitten for life. Occasional trips each season were his lot alongside numerous less meaningful excursions with his brother and dad to Spurs, until the 1977/78 season.

1978... ALAN, ALAN, ALAN AND LIAM

As Davies recalls, his Dad was keen to have his brother and him out of the house, but aged 11 he still deemed Alan too young to go on his own from Essex to North London. Obviously if Arsenal were at home, Tottenham were away, so his elder brother was reluctantly persuaded to take him to Highbury. There were four or five visits at the end of that season when Terry Neill was beginning to get a team together, all centred around Davies' first hero, Liam Brady

Davies still remembers the games well, but one that stood out was a 4-1 victory over Bristol City. Stapleton scored twice and Alan Sunderland was playing really well and got one as well. *"I liked him because he was called Alan obviously, even more when I realised he was called Alan Alan Alan Sunderland."*

Alan Alan Alan had been playing up front with Stapleton but lost his place when Arsenal's big name, big money striker, Malcom Macdonald, Supermac, returned from injury. Supermac played in the FA Cup Semi-Final and scored two in a 4-1 win over Orient. As Davies recalls neither shot was going in, took deflections and Macdonald claimed both. It was a day that was representative of the conflict in the Davies household.

He had been forced to go to White Hart Lane against his will with his brother to watch Tottenham play Bolton, a top of the table clash in the then Division Two; yes a league below Arsenal. Tottenham won 1-0 and pretty much secured promotion, but one of the three Davies' was more interested in the outcome of the Cup semi-final simultaneously being played at Stamford Bridge.

"So we got in the car to drive back and we turned Sports Report on, and before anything else was mentioned, they reported that Arsenal had won 3-0. So I was laughing and the pair of them were 'fucked off!'"

For a 12 year old Alan, having his team in the FA Cup final was massive; the bragging rights at school, the one-upmanship at home and the wonderful, long build up to the then traditional end of season television extravaganza. So the resultant loss to Ipswich hit him hard:

"I was devastated, and of course, I lived in a house where my dad and my older brother, who I never got on with, would go on about Tottenham all the bloody time and this was supposed to be it. We were going to win the Cup to shut them up,"

Davies recollects in some detail how Bobby Robson out-thought Terry Neill by playing Geddis on the right to nullify what was Arsenal's dominant left flank of Nelson, Rix and Brady. Of course, it was later revealed that Liam Brady, his hero, had not been fully fit and the day, 6 May 1978, that began with the promise of his first taste of Arsenal glory, ended with Davies sobbing into his pillow in his Loughton bedroom.

The Wembley disaster affected him so badly that Alan could not face going again with a gloating brother until the January of the following season. It was, of course, his hero Liam Brady that restored his faith in his team and the ability to face his brother again. Yes it was the moment from Arsenal's midfield genius that elicited the famous exuberant commentary from John Motson on the BBC "Look at that, oh look at that!" Brady's goal, the defining moment, in a pride restoring 5-0 victory over Arsenal's arch rivals and more importantly his brother's team.

"It was the Liam Brady goal against Tottenham in the 5-0 thrashing that propelled me back to Highbury. I wore a home-made badge with the date and score-line on under my school blazer lapel for months afterwards."

The win over Spurs was on 23 December 1978, and three weeks later, Davies convinced his brother to once again take him to Highbury. It was for the visit of the champions Nottingham Forest, and his brother was obviously keen to see Clough's great side and was convinced he would see Arsenal beaten.

"We used to go down the front in the West Lower and John Robertson scored early for Forest. I remember my brother turning to me and giving the fist clenched celebration, the fucker. We equalised with Price, then Stapleton got a winner and we beat them 2-1 in front of 52,000 it was just fucking amazing. I already loved it, but that was THE day. About six weeks later I turned 13 and my Dad said I could go on my own and I have just been going ever since."

AL OF AFC... A NORTH BANK REBEL

So, from the week he turned 13 and hit his teenage years, Alan Davies was free to break out from his comfortable suburban existence in commuter belt Loughton.

"My dad was an accountant and we went to public school. I hated it, it was a disaster. There were a few Arsenal people who said they supported them at the school but nobody who ever actually went."

Arsenal, and his new home of Highbury, were his release from the mundane. The number 20 bus from home to Walthamstow Central, and then the tube to Arsenal – *"This was my outlet, what I used to love and I went home and away on my own for pretty much ten years."*

This was also when his graffiti phase began, on which we compared notes. Whilst I was Dave HNB (Highbury North Bank) at around the same time, coming in from South East London, Davies was marking his own Gunner identity:

"I was 'Al of AFC woz here' then the date, so if you saw Al of AFC on a number 20 bus, that was me"

Aged 13, he loved Highbury more than anywhere he had been, and now, as a well-travelled adult, it is still his top spot. He feels that even as a grown up, when you look around; you will never find anywhere you love as much as your favourite childhood haunts. He moved from the School Boys' enclosure to the North Bank for the first time for the

final match of the 1980/81 season – a match, and a day, that he will never forget, for many reasons.

"The first time I went on the North Bank was the last game of the 1981 when we played Villa. There were about 57,000 and Arsenal won 2-0, but Villa still won the title because Ipswich did not get the result they need at Middlesbrough. I stood right at the back of the North Bank, and if you remember that day, Pele turned up in a suit for the match. He was paraded to the crowd and it was great to see him there. I was too young to have truly appreciated the 1970 World Cup [pictured above]. The whole of Highbury were singing 'Sign him up! Sign him up! Sign him up!' He was waving at the crowd and, at the end of the game, the whole crowd seemed to be on the pitch. All the Villa fans, the Clock End was swamped, it seemed like the whole of Birmingham had turned up. That was an amazing day."

Sold on the atmosphere, Davies was to remain on the North Bank for the next decade, until the end of the 1991 season. By then, he had met another comedian, Keith Dover (Tuesday Club), another comic mate Simon, and Patrick Marber, who was a comic writer and actor, but now a playwright and screenplay writer. So, when they announced that the North Bank was going to be knocked down at the end of 91/92 season, he moved to join his friends and they got four seats together in the West Lower.

"I did go back and stand on the North Bank one last time because I used to absolutely love it on there. I used to stand in the open bit

between the North and West. When it rained you would have to try and push your way under the stand. I used to stand next to the same crowd of blokes who would sing the players' songs literally every time each player touched the ball. If it was O' Leary it was 'David O'Leary' and when Rocky came into the side, every time he got the ball and dribbled, it was Oh Rocky Rocky!' Great memories."

MEETING ONE'S HEROES... LIAM 'CHIPPY' BRADY

Davies is no different to most Gooners of a certain age, and if your Arsenal journey began in the mid 1970's, a certain Irishman with a wand of a left foot was unparalleled. In 1979 Liam Brady was voted the best player in the league by his fellow professionals and the Red and White half of North London agreed. His finest season concluded so perfectly with his involvement in the move that won Arsenal the 1979 FA Cup Final. A year on, Davies was crying again at the final whistle, but this time the tears were of joy, and how perfect that Alan Alan Alan had scored the winner.

Davies was fortunate to meet the great man twice, but in very different circumstances; once as a teenager and once as an adult...

Surprisingly, his first chance meeting with his hero was in the upper tier at White Hart Lane where he had been dragged by his brother for a Spurs match with Manchester City. Their dad must have got the posh seats, because just along from where they were, was Irish international and Tottenham full back Jimmy Holmes, who was out injured, and sat with him, was his international colleague and friend, Liam Brady.

"My brother clocked him and said matter of factly; 'There's Liam Brady' and after that, he was all I could think about I knew I had to get his autograph. As soon as half time came I was over there, somehow I had a pen and I said 'Chippy' and that made him look. He was probably expecting 'Oh you Arsenal prick' from a Tottenham fan or something, but he signed my programme."

A couple of other kids went over to him, but he got up and went off for his half-term cuppa, so Davies was glad he had got in first and he has the autograph of his Arsenal idol on a Tottenham programme, which I guess is both cool and a nightmare at the same time. His nickname was Chippy apparently because he liked Chips. These days, of course, you would not be allowed chips anywhere near the training ground, or a footballer's diet, and his nickname, as Alan observes, would be *'Lightly Grilled Chicken!'*

Years later he got an e-mail from Comic Relief saying they were going to run a football team for a while and asking if he would play. There was to be a training session with the Arsenal, in the old indoor pitch at the Clock End, taken by Liam Brady. Alan wasn't playing any football at the time, and by his own admission, is not a very good footballer, but he was not likely to turn down such an invite.

"So I got up there and it was obvious that Brady did not really want to run a training session. He wanted us to have a game, eight-a-side of whatever against the under 15s. So I said to him 'You are having a laugh Liam?' I wasn't good enough to play against them when I was 15, I was thinking, and I was fucked!"

"So first of all he warmed us up and had us running across the pitches. You know, six crossings or whatever you call them. I was up for it, super keen and up the front because it's Liam Brady my childhood hero but, by the end (and fuck me I was knackered) I was thinking 'are going to play now?' Then we set off again and about three in to the eight crossings I was on my back. Brady says to me 'flattered to deceive there Alan!' So now he was putting me down in front of everyone!"

After some more stretching under his watchful eye Brady then brought out the Arsenal under 15s. Davies describes the almost complete and utter embarrassment that ensued as he and his team mates were 6-0 down in about ten minutes.

On the infrequent occasion when Davies or another colleague actually managed to get the ball and trying to pass it, as you watched it heading to whomever you thought you were passing to, a red and white blur had nipped in and intercepted it. Davies's astute football brain had spotted the problem…

"Brady played at the back. So when he got possession the two fullbacks just fucked off to the sides, someone dropped in from midfield, he knocked into him and they would ping it wide, they were so well drilled. So I thought we have got to get to the source of this. Brady is the problem for us here, he is pulling the strings. I'll go and close him down," (At the point Davies is laughing uncontrollably as he recounts this, as am I.)

"So I ran towards him, he was the last man and he slipped up, I took the ball and I thought I was in on goal. But then he picks his left foot up, suspended it over the ball and just sort of flicked it and whilst I am watching, hypnotised by that foot, as I had been for years as a kid, he then whipped the ball away and passed it to one of his lads. It was an absolute joy."

photo courtesy of Stuart Macfarlane and Arsenal FC

Davies hosting the AFC Foundation Ball

MEETING ONE'S HEROES... ARSENE WENGER

Alan Davies is a huge admirer of Wenger and this is born not just out of respect for his achievements. He has been fortunate enough to meet Arsenal's longest serving manager on a few occasions, and sitting close to the home dug out at the Emirates, finds himself fascinated by observing the man during matches.

For all his life in entertainment and comedy Davies is convinced he has never met anyone quite like Arsene Wenger – nobody as 'Guru' like as the Arsenal boss. On occasions he is asked by the club to host Q&A sessions, usually for fan groups and normally, he jokes, when Tom Watt is not available. He has found it difficult to concentrate on his role at these events because he finds listening to Wenger almost hypnotic

"You find yourself just sitting listening to his answers to the questions and thinking there should be a 'Little Red Book of Arsene' like Chairman Mao's."

Alan is particularly fascinated with the Frenchman's understanding of human nature and the vulnerability to emotional stress. As Davies recalls, Wenger says; *'You have got to keep your emotions in line with your ambitions. If you know where you want to go, but your emotions waiver, it makes you ambition vulnerable.'* Wenger demonstrates this visually with his fingers as having to be able to control your emotions, so you are all pointing in the same direction.

It is why Davies tells me, that Wenger has this thing about calmness and quiet in the dressing room. This is all about his players, in theory, learning to be able to control their emotions at all times, so that when it comes to the crucial moment in the game, they will be relaxed. For Wenger, as he relates, it's not about the will to win, as the Frenchman assumes that if you have got to a first team squad level at Arsenal, it is taken for granted. You are going to be that sort of intense person having made it that far.

This is why, as Davies explains, Wenger hates the style of manager who is frantic and busy on the touchline. For him this only serves to betray your own anxiety, and that will transfer to his players. This philosophy originated from his time managing in Japan, where Wenger told him, there was no point shouting at the Japanese players. It is built into the very fabric of the Japanese to always follow instruction and always do so to the absolute best of their ability. Therefore, if you then shout at them, they just get perplexed and upset –'don't shout at us, just tell us what to do and we will do it!' Wenger's time in The J League moulded him into the style of manager he is, and as Davies understands, not all British supporters can relate to that.

"As a British fan, you often want your manager to be like you, to jump up and down, show their emotion and demonstrate they care as you do. If I was down there I would be doing this, that and the other, but he doesn't want anyone doing that."

Sitting behind the dug-out and technical area Davies senses that, on occasion, Wenger now trusts Stevie Bould to shout instruction, but in the past, he has often seen him put his arm across Rice and others as if to say 'I don't want us yelling in the technical area, it's not what we're about.' Before actually meeting 'Le Professeur', and having the benefit of having the philosophy explained, Davies thinks it was the FA Cup Semi Final in 1998 when he realised Wenger was different.

"The game that sticks in my mind is when we played Wolves at Villa Park in the FA Cup Semi-final in 1998. We had a good view and I watched Wenger walk down to the dug-out and he just looked so relaxed. It was a semi-final, the place was absolutely full of black and gold balloons, thousands of them, the Wolves fans were taking the roof off and you knew they were going to come out pumped. I was thinking we are going to have to match them early doors otherwise we could get blown away and Wenger just sauntered out with his hands in his pockets and I thought he did not look up for it. Why was he not looking excited or nervous, but of course you knew underneath he must be churning away, desperate to win his first trophy in English football. Then of course the team came out full of composure and confidence, without Bergkamp, and created chances from the off and got the job done. I realised then that was his style."

Inevitably there are occasions when even Arsene Wenger allows his calmness to slip. We will all recall him kicking the water bottle at Old Trafford, for example, or when he pushed Mourinho on the touch-line. Such lapses, for Davies, are rare, but he recounts beautifully and amusingly a recent match that encapsulates both the Wenger philosophy perfectly, and indeed, when the façade disappeared.

"When we played Manchester City recently (December 2015) he and Pellegrini was similar and it was like they had a 'casual off' in their technical areas. They both strolled around with their hands in their pockets. The game was intense, huge, and with a worldwide audience. Everything about his philosophy, face to face with the side he probably sees as the arch criminals, the fucking cheats who will ruin football, everything he has hated his whole career. To him, they have done it the wrong way and he is facing them down in the ground that he built, with the team that plays the way he wants to play."

"Like a fucking Zen Master, like Yoda in Stars Wars who had to show them how it should be done – I am thinking he is going to get a fucking light sabre out in a minute. This is it, this is everything about him – I am calm, I am relaxed, my team play the beautiful game in a beautiful ground that is designed for pleasure and art. I built it you twat!

"Of course Pellegrini has got a swagger about him too, the front man of this billion-dollar corporation and it was fascinating. Then Yaya Toure scored, who was the boy that he had rejected after one game at Barnet, and he would have watched subsequently play all round Europe, setting records and winning medals. He stuck that goal in, and what a goal, then fuck me the gloves were off. He is agitated, he is kicking every ball,

image by Dawit Sissay

An Alan Davies perspective of Wenger?

and he is jumping around all over the technical area. When he was two up he was his Zen like self and fine but he could not sustain it. So it is in there, but he tries to keep a lid on it for his philosophy.

Another aspect high on Davies' list of things to admire about Wenger is that he considers himself a teacher who has the ultimate responsibility to the boys he brings through, and to make sure it works out for them, whether at Arsenal or elsewhere.

"He would never fuck you up; he would never do what George Graham did to Paul Davis and put him in the reserves for a year and a half. He would never sell a player over a disagreement, but he would let a player go if it was right for their career and he could not offer progression."

Sometimes the decisions can hurt you as a fan because, for Davies and for most of us as fans, we love nothing more than to see one of our own succeeding. It is why we all have so much of ourselves vested in Jack Wilshere. Davies offers Steve Sidwell as the perfect example of a player who had been at the club for 12 years when sold to Reading, and he would have sooner seen him playing in the Red and White than Flamini. However, Wenger made the decision for the betterment of Sidwell's career and was proved correct. He adds the recent decision to sell Benik Afobe to Wolves. As an Arsenal supporter, when you now see him back in the Premier League, charging around and scoring for Bournemouth, you cannot help but feel a pang of regret, but again, Wenger would not hold the young man back.

AWAY DAY SCRAPES AND JOLLY JAPES

Davies' insight on Wenger was fascinating and quite intense, so by contrast, he chose to share some amusing memories of his younger days on the road with his team. He was a regular away supporter as a teenager and he is clear, as was his friend Ian Stone, that in the 1980s, it could often be quite harrowing, and on occasion, terrifying to follow Arsenal on the road. It was what you did to support your team, but looking back, there were so many narrow escapes after matches, being chased back to the coaches and hiding in gardens and alley ways. However, surprisingly, Davies has only been punched once at an Arsenal match, and it was by a fellow Gooner, which he describes as 'pretty annoying'.

He would travel away, often with the Arsenal Travel Club. He fondly recalls, with irony, how they used to walk up the aisle on the coach with a bin bag full of sweaty rolls throwing them at you to catch. One such occasion was a trip to Elm Park, Reading, for an FA Cup Third Round tie in January 1987. This was the day Davies was hit by another Arsenal way fan, and the cause that day and the root of all evil, was fences.

"It was raining and the away, end was only about 50 deep, it was a tiny terrace. So all of us were in there and a fence, and I hate fuck-

ing fences. *We all know what killed people at Hillsborough, it was the fences and it is the people who said that you had to play semi-finals with fences that should be in fucking prison. We escaped tragedies at Highbury because we refused to put them up."*

That day at Elm Park there were a lot of drunk blokes on a tiny terrace that was hardly ever, if ever, full, with insufficient barriers. Davies was near the front and the fans behind were surging down and there were kids and mums that were getting crushed up against the fences.

"One mum was saying 'stop pushing please there's kids here' and they surged again and I am on my own so I turned round and pushed this bloke behind me saying 'fuck off there's a load of kids down here'. And he fucking hit me! I couldn't believe it, there's all these kids. So I grabbed hold of him and we are wrestling about with each other and then people are pulling us apart. Some bloke said to me 'it's not worth it mate' although they didn't do it again, I went home with a massive shiner by my eye!"

For a reason best known to himself, certainly nothing to do with fashion, Davies used to wear a bright orange coat with a hood in the early 90s. In the spring of 1991, with the Gunners pushing for the title, Davies and his friends were making the away trip to Bramall Lane, Sheffield. As was often the case in those early days of trying to forge a career as a stand-up, he had a random gig up north, so was going to meet his friends at the ground. A vague, none too optimistic arrangement was made to meet somewhere behind the goal. The team's away following tends to swell when a team is going for the league, and there were thousands of Gooners there as Davies made his way in and positioned himself, unhopefully, behind the goal.

"We had the whole end virtually so I get in there and think there is literally no way I am going to find them in here. Then I got a tap on the shoulder and there they are. You can imagine can't you. It's like 'waaaaaaaeeeh!! How the fuck did you find me?' 'You got a bright orange coat on you berk we spotted you a mile off; you look like a bloody steward!'"

A month later the 90/91 title was all but secured with a 0-0 draw against Sunderland at Roker Park, with Liverpool having lost earlier in the day to Chelsea. For Davies, the stand out memory was the warmth shown by one Sunderland fan after the game, particularly as the point was not enough for his own team in their fight to avoid the drop.

"At the end of the game, after most of the ground had cleared, a Sunderland fan walked across the terrace so he could get to where we

all were. He had his kid with him who must have been about eight. He just came up and was shaking all our hands saying 'You've won the fooking league lads; you've won the fooking league."

Davies recalls that all the Arsenal fans were simply in awe of the 'football family' gesture made by this guy in the face of his own team's relegation.

Some of the best memories from football are provided on the pitch, but equally, many that stand out are the comedic episodes with friends. A stand out recollection for Davies, and one that still makes him laugh out loud today, was on his 27th birthday, in March 1993. He and three mates had piled into his old Vauxhall Cavalier that had made many an away trip. One of their number was Alan's mate Simon, a young stand-up comedian, and not to put too fine a point on it, a big lad who liked his food. It came as no surprise to any of them that, part way into the journey, Simon declared he was peckish and in need of a snack.

"There are four of us and somewhere on the A12 my mate Simon declares he needs a snack, he is a big lad, so we stop at some services. So he gets out and we are all in the car just sitting there waiting, while he is inside checking out the pasties, or whatever. He comes out of the shop and we all watch him walk across the forecourt and he gets into someone else's car. It's fucking hilarious because he is huge. The idea that somebody look around to find some random bloke in an Arsenal hat! The door shut, then about half a second later, it flew open and he jumped out. Of course we are all pissing ourselves. We won 4-2 that day and Tony Adams headed one in with a plaster over his eye because he had fallen down the stairs the night before."

It was wonderful to chat with Alan Davies and to explore the origins of his love for the Arsenal – I could have listened to his reminiscences all day.

NOTHING FINER THAN AN ARSENAL ONE LINER!

This book will be true to its aim, to explore support of the UK's top comedic talent whose allegiance is to the famous the Red and White of the Arsenal. It fast became apparent that some funny men are very serious about their football and others are just seriously funny. The result is happily a rich variety of style and outcome from person to person and chapter to chapter.

I guess what we have to remember is that comedy is a job and football is a passion and not all comedians are, or want to be, funny off stage or screen. As the subject of this particular chapter, Milton Jones, told Sian Ranscombe at *The Telegraph* in February 2015.

"There are two types of comedian: the one who is on all the time and the one who is playing a role. If you're in a band, people want to hear the old songs, but they don't want to hear the old jokes." *

Armed with this wisdom I asked that we might conduct the interview in the style of a 1970's *Shoot* Q&A and that the answers be fired back in the mode of the Milton Jones that the nation knows and loves. So, prepare yourself for wackiness, the famed one liners and a slightly leftfield quick-fire exploration of Milton Jones, the Gooner.

So Milton can you tell the readers about the origins of your support for the Gunners?

"In the spring of '71 I was under pressure in the playground to pick a team to support. That night on BBC Nationwide I saw an item about some supporters knitting a very long red and white scarf to support Arsenal in the Cup Final. I decided there and then, without seeing a ball kicked. So, originally, I suppose I was more a fan of scarves."

How old were you when you first got to see the team live and what do you recall about the occasion?

"I only got to see the Gunners on TV for years. It wasn't until 1991 that I saw the Championship trophy brought to Highbury before beating Manchester United 3-1."

So who have been your Arsenal heroes through the years and perhaps why?

"Charlie George initially, he fell over when he scored in the '71 cup final. I thought that was hilarious. Then Alan Ball, he had white boots. Next Liam Brady who was only little but could dribble and bend the ball. Then Thierry, of course, and now Alexis Sanchez, who has had way too much coffee I think!"

I have read that you play football these days with other comedians? How did that come about and please name drop. I am guessing there may be fellow Gooners who play given how many there seem to be (thankfully for this book project.)

"Not as much as I used to, but comedians have played in all sorts of kick-arounds and charity games over the years. Russell Howard and John Bishop are the best known ones. Lee Mack is a goal-hanger. I play like a sensible Paul Merson. A lot of comedians support Arsenal, probably because they laughed when they first heard the word said out loud."

I won't go on about your status as 'King of the One Liner' but if you have any football, or even Arsenal ones, appropriate for this interview I will be extremely chuffed.

"I got most abuse for saying that 'Tottenham are like a burglar in prison, because there'll be no silverware without Bale.' This one you'll like, 'the match I really want to see is Alex Ferguson's Manchester United v North Korea's Arsenal'. Oh yes and I've always wanted to put a team together with the likes of Cantona, di Canio and Roy Keane in it and call it Real Sociopath."

I have seen you on Ian Stone's 'The Football's On' show so do you enjoy chatting football as so many of us do?

"There's something cathartic about talking about something passionately with blokes. But it's very easy to end up re-hashing what you've already heard from other pundits. At the end of the day (there's another cliché) none of us know the whole story do we? Who is really carrying an injury, how bad someone's been in training etc."

You have three children so have you managed to indoctrinate any of them?

"My eldest son supports the right team and it was a real bucket list moment to go with him to the 2014 Cup Final against Hull – if a slightly stressful match!"

You buy retro, garish shirts and it has become a trademark look on TV, but do you have any retro Arsenal shirts or are you not a shirt-wearing fan?

"I've got a 70's short-sleeved red and white classic, an 80's JVC special and a knock off Hong Kong blue third kit with 'Reyes' on the back. I got my first kit when I was seven. My brother supported Leeds but he got a Chelsea kit because it would be 'easier to wash'. We still laugh about this. Well, only me to be fair."

TRUSTEE LONG SERVING SEVENTIES RETRO

How often, with your busy schedule, do you get to see the Arsenal and do you have a season ticket?

"I only get to go two or three times a season maybe. This is due to touring and working in the evenings – and not trusting Sky or BT to change the timings! Having a season ticket would spoil me and be quite stressful."

I would be quite intrigued to know how you feel about the crowds and the language in the stadium. I read that as a Christian, for you personally that means swearing and blaspheming are out, but for your peers, friends and a high percentage of football match goers, I assume it is very much in?

"Sometimes swearing can be very creative. Also people can be obnoxious without swearing. In general I think God is more concerned with general attitudes rather than individual words. I don't swear in my act in order to be as accessible to as many people as possible, and not to rely on an unnecessary crutch."

So back on to the Arsenal, which is the best team that you have seen and why?

"Well, by definition, The Invincibles can't be beaten. But I think some of George Graham's early teams over-achieved magnificently."

Care to also comment on some of the worst players and times?

"Nick Hornby in Fever Pitch talks about Gus Caesar being awful for us, but also how he was still way, way better than any of us watching. That sums it up really. Like many, I get more cross with players who have loads of ability, but for whatever reason, seem to stop trying such as Arshavin, Adebayor etc"

Are there any particularly amusing memories, Arsenal related? Trips away perhaps or compromising situations?

"At the time of the 'Anfield miracle' I was on a charity trip to Africa surrounded by disinterested church volunteers who were more preoccupied with feeding the hungry. They didn't seem notice that something really important had happened!"

Has your celebrity afforded you any special memories or treats from the club? Have you, for example, met any of the managers or players on match days or perhaps been asked to host club events?

"I have avoided meeting, or doing shows, for Arsenal players and staff in case they clearly don't like what I do. This would taint my supporting experience. I did meet Pat Jennings at London Airport once, but that was when he played for Spurs. I like to think that was the beginning of his defection!"

I am deliberately keeping off the present team and manager as you are aware of the divide in our fan base. However, if you would like to comment on the present regime and manager please do.

"When Arsene finally goes up to the great dugout in the sky where his anorak zip will finally be fixed forever, it will probably be a Princess Diana moment for a lot of people. They will suddenly see what he has done in context – how the club has gone from being like a second hand Land Rover to temperamental Maserati – and I know which I would rather watch race!"

Nearly there I think Milton, but if you have any more football anecdotes of note before we wrap up?

"A few years ago I was playing the Manchester Apollo and a group of people came in during the first half. It turned out to be Mario Balotelli and his entourage, but they were supposed to have been at a rap gig down the road and left at the interval. I like to think it was his loss!"

Before you go I must of course ask you to name your all time Arsenal XI based on the players you have actually watched. A few words if you have a dilemma on a selection perhaps and ideally tell me the formation you would like your team to play?

Ozil – they say he can play anywhere – let's see if he can play in goal
Jennings – never used his hands anyway.
Sanchez – would be a very annoying full back
O'Leary – went on to present X Factor
Bould – should've shaved his head and worn eyeliner while still playing.
Alan Ball – I had a ball called Alan once
Abou Diaby – at least he'd get a game
Liam Brady – imagine him feeding Henry
Thierry Henry – imagine him being fed by Brady
Dennis Bergkamp – coolest man ever called Dennis
Sanchez again – has got the energy to play in two positions
Kanu – like an unpredictable tree
4, 3, 3 Dave

Thanks Milton it's been enlightening!

CHRIS MARTIN... MAKING UP FOR LOST TIME

I think if you spent an hour or so in the company of one of Britain's most promising young observational comedians, you would expect to laugh. Sharing a coffee with Chris Martin (no not the singer) I most certainly did, out loud. He has an infectious charisma and is simply fun to be around, but boy is he a pathetic excuse for a Gunner! Well at least that is what Chris feels because, although not quite thirty, he was (self admittedly) very late to his own Arsenal party. So, when beginning the interview with *'So where did it all begin for you with Arsenal, Chris?',* I was not expecting this answer:

"Well I think people will just call me a shit fan but I have an unusual backstory!"

SAVED FROM MAN UNITED BY GRANDAD

In truth I doubt they will as we all have differing journeys to our love affairs with Arsenal, and we cannot all be born in North London with fanatical Arsenal mad families, can we?

In essence, being born in West London with parents who had not even the vaguest interest in football, Martin had to find it for himself. Despite arriving on this earth in the summer of 1986, when a new era was dawning at Highbury, Christopher Martin was oblivious to the impending glory in N5. At school, as was the way in those days, and sadly still can be today, kids followed recently successful teams. The primary school playground initiation was Panini football stickers and a choice, it seemed, to support either Liverpool or Manchester United. Funnily enough we will return to the hatred of Liverpool FC and to

football stickers later, but Martin, who was overwhelmed by Liverpool love amongst his 'glory hunting' four and five year old peers, opted for Man United. Don't worry this awful phase was not real and it took an elderly relative to show young Chris the error of his ways.

Aged six it dawned on Chris that whilst his parents were no help at all with his spiritual guidance, his Grandad, who had Parkinson's disease, was a massive Arsenal fan. So, after a year or two of vaguely supporting United just to have something to say in the playground, he suddenly thought 'what the hell am I doing?' There was no real connection with Manchester and, as he lived in Harlesden, logic suggested a London team, but it was a moving episode with his Grandad that brought home what should have been staring him in the face.

"It was a weird, but oddly strong, bond that I had with my grandad. He could not communicate too well with me but he understood me and I must have mentioned football as I was chattering away. He then reached behind himself and took an Arsenal scarf from the back of his chair and handed it to me. I was moved I guess, as much as a six year old would be and thought, of course, I should be supporting this team and it made so much more sense."

NEWCASTLE, NO SEX AND BACK

Even then, with his proud new status at school as an Arsenal supporter, there was no one to truly encourage him in this support or give him the impetus to try and work out how to get to a game. So it was not until he was in his teens, and at senior school, that he really got into the Gunners.

"I am a late blooming Arsenal fan. My first game was at Craven Cottage (15/9/2001) we won 3-1 and Bergkamp scored a sumptuous side footer, placed in the top corner from the edge of the box to seal the win. I was taken by a friend and was in the Fulham end. I knew I loved Arsenal, but in no time, I was off to University in Newcastle, so I was disassociated again."

Ironically, at Newcastle University, about as far from London as he could be, from 2005 to 2008 Martin feels he truly became obsessed with Arsenal. When I asked why, it seems there may have been two main factors

"I think it was because everyone I knew started having a girlfriend, but I did not get one until I was 26 – I honestly think I became obsessed with Arsenal because I had no sex life!"

He recalls coming home from Newcastle in the holidays and all his mates at home would say 'when did you become such a huge Arsenal fan?' He was certainly a late blooming supporter and it seems the second factor, that deepened his Gooner identity at the beginning of the barren years, was that at University he shared digs with three Liverpool fans.

"None of those three were from Liverpool, which just summed it all up really and reaffirmed it for me. So basically I got truly into Arsenal when we were shit and stopped winning things, so maybe I am a true fan after all!"

University is like that, a time when one accentuates character traits and one's identity. For Chris Martin, living with three pseudo Liverpool supporters served to ensure he became further pronounced in his London Arsenal persona. It was also where he began to try out early comedy routines including reaching the finals of the 'Chortle Student Comedian of the Year in 2005.

"Arsenal became an obsession. I didn't have any hobbies apart from comedy, which became a job, and Arsenal. Every day I would check the Arsenal blogs and wanted to learn everything. I don't know why I didn't have that obsession at school, or why it came so late to me, but in my early 20s I was totally into Arsenal. Like a good wine I guess!"

THE HIGHBURY REGRET AND EMIRATES BET

Martin's late development as a 'proper fan' gives cause to one of his great Arsenal regrets – that he never got to see his team play at their spiritual home, Highbury. He feels that although he has made up for lost time at the Emirates, he's only experienced a 'sanitised' version of watching The Arsenal.

"I know it is just not the same and the people who sometimes sit around me annoy me so much for not showing the same passion I show, or want to show."

Martin does not really have any friends who share his passion, other than those in his profession, and we all know now, if we did not already, that there are plenty of like-minded comedians. In 2012/13 he hooked up with fellow stand-up Rob Beckett, with two borrowed season tickets. That was the first season he was a regular. It is extremely difficult with a job that frequently has you on the road and working evenings, but he had begged and borrowed seats before this and is also on the waiting list.

Of course getting single tickets can mean going on your own. It should not matter because we are all Gooners together, but Martin bemoans the fact that he always seemed to end up next to a grumpy old bugger. He feels when Arsenal score he should be able to hug the stranger next to him with no inhibitions, but he has seldom felt inclined. Although he recalls he did do so when Arshavin scored the winner against Barcelona in 2011.

"I paid £150 and could not think of a better way to have spent the money. That was one of the top live moments for me when Arshavin scored."

He sometimes goes with a pal who has memberships in Club Level, which he appreciates but does not enjoy watching his football from the posh seats as much. He is forever sat behind a bloke who slags off a particular player for the whole 90 minutes. He would rather be in the cheap seats where he was in 2012/13 with Beckett. He was right next to the away fans, where it may not have been the best view for the whole match, but the atmosphere, banter and singing was amazing.

The season he and Beckett had the loaned season tickets gave him many happy and amusing memories – one of his favourite anecdotes relates to a passionate Arsenal fan who always wore a pink Nike hoodie. I hope he reads this book because Chris Martin remembers your antics with affection and you are a legend to him. In short, this guy got removed by the stewards every single match for being overly abusive to the visiting away fans.

"Depending on how early the game kicked off would depend how pissed he was and how early he got kicked out. So, if it was a lunchtime kick off, he would make it to about the 80th minute before the stewards moved in, a three o'clocker 'til about the 60th minute, but at 5.30, he was gone just after half-time. He would get so excited when we scored, and was so passionate it was always a shame to see him go, but he was forever issuing death threats! It was his routine: Get tanked up; Go to Arsenal; Go mental; Abuse the opposition fans; Get kicked out!"

The first game Rob and Chris went to together was against Southampton – Arsenal thrashed them 6-1. Rob obviously felt confident as it was only newly promoted Saints there would be no bother, so he wore his Arsenal shirt. Martin has never worn a shirt to a match since he wore one and Arsenal lost at home, a fan superstition thing.

"After the game we were walking out, just chatting to each other, and straight outside the exit there were five Southampton fans who shouted 'Shut up you Mong' to Rob. I am not sure if they recognised him, or if it was just the first person out in a shirt, but Rob said 'I may not wear this shirt next week!'

That season Martin was also there for what he describes as one of the best days of his life, which was the second successive Arsenal 5 Spurs 2 affair. It was a very early date with his new girlfriend, now wife, Hannah. On a whim, he stopped on the concourse and placed a £2 bet on Arsenal to win 5-2, explaining to his bemused date what had happened the previous season. It was 100-1 for a reason, but could lightening possibly strike twice at the Emirates?

Chris and Hannah celebrating at the Emirates

"She had never been to a football game before, and until recently, had not been to one since. I said to her you will probably never see a match like that again. So she came to the second 5-2, I won £200 and the girl turned out to be the one for me. It was the best day of my life. Moments like that are what it's all about."

PARTNER IN LIFE, FOOTBALL AND FIFA

It was ultimately a blessing because ever since Hannah totally understands her partner's obsession and even supports him in it. The truth is that she finds the whole thing funny in the extreme:

"Hannah finds it hilarious that I never ever get angry with her about anything but when Giroud misses a sitter, I jump around and slap and punch the wall and stuff. I don't know what it is I think it was because Arsenal was my girlfriend for many years and now it is still someone I am seeing on the side."

Not only does his wife seem to understand his passion, and find it amusing, but what is definitely strange, and what may make thousands of men jealous, is that Hannah actually enjoys watching her husband play FIFA!

"I remember when were in a cab in Scotland a few years back and I said to her how weird it was that she enjoyed watching me play FIFA. She said 'I just really like watching it, it is like a film.' The cabbie turned round and said in a broad Scottish accent 'Sorry I overheard the conversation and if you don't mind me saying, you have to be the greatest woman on Earth, can I marry you?"

Sadly, for the Glaswegian cabbie, Chris and Hannah were married late in 2015 and spent a long honeymoon in the Philippines as she is half Filipino. It transpired that a family friend in Manila was a mad Arsenal fan too, and part of a small community of likeminded individuals who had set up the Philippines Arsenal Supporters Club in 2009. They congregate at Heckle and Jeckle Sports Bar for the matches, and the newlyweds made their way there via a precarious walk through the Red Light District to see Arsenal entertain Chelsea.

"We lost 1-0 to Chelsea but the atmosphere was better than it often is at the Emirates. They knew all the chants and it was a blast."

Hannah's second trip was on Valentine's Day 2016 and ended in that last minute winner against Leicester – it would be fair to say the Emirates crowd, including Chris and Hannah, went pretty mad that day.

AND BACK TO LIVERPOOL FANS

Returning to a recurring theme that began at primary school, and reared its ugly head again at university, it seems that those irritating Liverpool fans won't leave him be. Chris found himself watching the 2014 FA Cup Final in a Casino in Auckland, before the New Zealand Comedy Festival – he was with a Kiwi comic who supported Arsenal. The two Gooners were sitting watching the build-up, minding their own business, but as Chris observes, "wherever you go on this earth it seems there is always an annoying Scouse Liverpool fan!"

"There were quite a few other Arsenal fans, but this guy, of course had to pick on me. He came up to me before the kick-off and said 'Wenger's got to go' which immediately needled me, so I said 'who are you?' and he said it again; 'Wenger's not good enough, he's got to go.' I was like 'whatever mate' and then at two-nil down he popped back in my face; 'Wenger's got to go hasn't he?'

Chris hanging out with the Philippines Gooners

I was thinking 'Oh my God I hate you!' Cazorla got one back and obviously I wanted us to break our trophy drought but I REALLY wanted to get in the Scouser's face. At two each he was still there; 'Still not good enough, he has got to go.' So when Ramsey scored I literally leapt up and jumped into his face... 'Does he have to go, does he really have to go?!!'

It was such an exciting moment and I wished he was near me every time we got to a final. "There's nothing that makes Arsenal winning better than giving a Scouser some shit!"

THE MILT CUP

Chris supported Milton (Jones) on tour for virtually the whole of 2013. Milton got a mobile broadband router in the tour car so, that wherever they went, they could watch the Arsenal games on stream when being driven to the shows. The two football nuts invented a thing called the 'Milt Cup' in which they competed with each other.

"We had two little football goals, and at each venue, we would place them at either end of a corridor and would play first to ten with a ball. I would always wear my yellow JVC 'Ian Wright' shirt and he would wear

an *Eighties red and white JVC one. We played at every theatre and at the end of the tour I won, which is the main thing!"*

He told me that Milton is actually a good footballer though – and very competitive. He also informed me that Jones is a goal hanger who never passes, and interestingly, Tim Vine is the same, which gives rise to a Martin theory;

"I have worked it out that one-liner comedians like to goal hang and just put it in. It is like their comedy style, straight to the punchline."

Martin describes it as an honour, and brilliant fun, to go on tour with Milton. They became good pals, but he finds it slightly strange due to the age difference. *"We are mates, but in my head, he is like my Dad!"* The fact that Milton often has his family and kids with him, and never swears, brings to mind another funny story. One night he was back stage, in the dressing room with Milton, when Chris got an email from his Comedy Podcast partner, Spurs lover and close friend, Carl Donnelly, which simply had a one line message – 'Hey man, I have got a really great holiday photo for you.'

"So I opened the photo and there was three Zulu warriors with massive boners. So I started laughing like a maniac, but in my head, it was even funnier and harder to control because I felt naughty because Milton was there. So, of course, he wanted to know what's so funny and I am like 'Trust me Milton, you don't want to know, but he is like 'come on!' Finally I showed him and he said 'Why would someone do that?'"

Chris justifies telling me this story for the book on the grounds that it was an evil Tottenham fan (and more of him later,) causing him to feel naughty in front of his Arsenal comedy Dad. Tenuous, but funny, which leads us to Chris Martin's final story from our whistle stop tour of his Arsenal memory bank.

EVIL COKE AND PANINI STICKERS

Before anyone thinks this story includes snorting illegal narcotics through rolled up football stickers, let me allay your concerns, as it does not. It does, however, involve evil crime, theft, deception and revenge. They say revenge is sweet and, in this case, the revenge was Chris Martin's for a crime inflicted upon him some 25 years ago.

First we must journey back to Falcon's Primary school where a mis-guided, as yet unenlightened by Grandad, Man United supporting Chris Martin was collecting football stickers. The stickers were banned from the school, but he had still taken his in, which was a grave error. Another guy in his class, Giles Coke, who Martin had considered a mate, stole all his stickers.

"It was only me and him who had taken them in, so I confronted him and said 'Have you stolen my stickers Giles?' to which he responded 'Yes but you are not supposed to have them here, so who are you going to tell?' I thought you evil genius. I moved schools about a year later and forgot about him."

Years later, in 2010, Martin saw an announcement on Sky Sports News saying that a Giles Coke had signed for Sheffield Wednesday from Motherwell. Could it be the same football sticker thief, as it was not a common name? Some investigation confirmed that the professional footballer, and Panini burglar, was indeed one and the same person. Further evidence Martin felt at the time of life's unfairness. A few years later he told the story on his podcast and listeners then started tweeting Giles saying 'give Chris Martin his football stickers back!'

"Coke replied and asked these Tweeters what they were talking about – to which I thought classic Giles Coke, deny, deny deny! So I stepped in and Tweeted him saying they were just being silly because about 20 years ago at school you stole my stickers, don't you remember? He said he didn't."

"So, after a short conversation, I said look I am supporting Milton Jones on a national tour and we are coming to Sheffield would you like a couple of tickets for the show and he said yeah thanks. So when it was getting near to the show I got a tweet from him asking what happened about my tickets for the show and I replied: 'What Show?' Revenge felt so sweet for Chris!

HAS HE MADE UP FOR LOST TIME?

A self-confessed late comer to his Arsenal obsession, I think we are left in no doubt that Chris Martin is making up for lost time as a Gooner. Sadly we cannot transport him back to Highbury, but if it is not obvious by now, to assist the case for the defence of him *not* 'being a pathetic excuse for a Gooner', I'll leave you with one last remark from Chris:

"I can't wait to have a son. My Dad wasn't into football, but I will be there, waiting, ready to put him in an Arsenal shirt as he comes out of the vagina – ready to catch him with my Arsenal towel." (Sorry Hannah!)

You are not a shit fan Chris!

CLIVE ANDERSON... WHOSE TEAM IS IT ANYWAY?

Barrister turned comedian, Clive Anderson, pretty much *was* Channel 4 from about the height of George Graham at Arsenal, until well after Wenger's first Double. He hosted ten seasons of the fabulous improvisational panel comedy show *Whose Line is it anyway?* as well as fronting his own chat show *Clive Anderson Talks Back* for a similar period. His quick tongue and instant wit was honed at Cambridge University where being President of the Footlights, saw him as the first act on stage at the Leicester Square's famous Comedy Store. It was from that hotbed of new comedy and improvisation that he drew many of the stars of his hit show, which he took from radio to television in 1988.

Looking back, it is hard not to see his work as ground-breaking, when you consider the comedy panel shows so popular today – particularly *Mock the Week*. More often these days he is a guest and not the host, but I feel sure many of the younger panellists, some of whom feature in the chapters of this book, are tipping their hat to Anderson and thanking him.

Whilst his keen intellect, razor sharp humour and easy fast-talking charm have taken Anderson from the bar, to stand-up, to radio and television on both sides of the Atlantic in a career spanning more than 35 years, his love affair with the Arsenal began over 55 years ago.

So where did it all start for the man, who when asked in 2015 in a broadsheet interview what his greatest fear was, replied; *"Arsenal conceding from a corner."* (*Guardian* with Rosanna Greenstreet, 20/06/15).

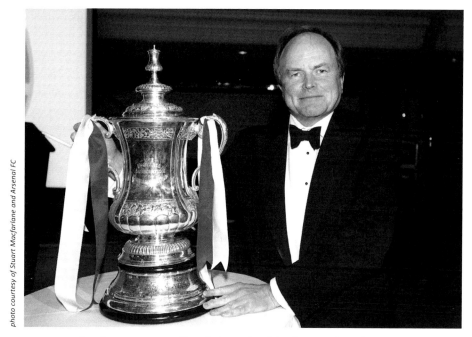

**Anderson proudly pictured with the FA Cup in 2005
at the AFC Foundation Ball**

THE SIXTIES

Football loomed large in his childhood, with his father, a Glaswegian, full of tales of the mighty Rangers. Although born in Stanmore, Middlesex, Anderson dodged the ignominy of supporting the 'Middlesex team' because his football fanatical father had fortuitously resided in Highbury before and after the war.

"I suppose Watford, Chelsea or even Tottenham might have been equally close to where I lived, but luckily the suggestion of supporting them never arose. I believe 1961 was a big year for Tottenham, but we instinctively knew it was to be a flash in the pan."

His first trips to the 'Home of Football' were in the 1961/62 season, and whilst he does not recollect the first two visits, aside from the awe he felt, it was the third trip to Highbury that has stayed with him to this day. It was Arsenal v Blackpool on 7th October 1961, when Anderson was eight years old, that is etched in his memory. It was so memorable as it was to be Stanley Matthews' last match at Highbury. He was already in his forties and was going to be leaving Blackpool, then in the First Division, to return to Stoke at the end of the season. But, as it turned out, the match was to be Matthews' last ever appearance in a Blackpool shirt.

"Some of the historic nature of it all must have been explained to me by father and my friend's father, as we watched it from an awkward position on the terracing above the corner flag between the North Bank and the East Stand. We never stood there before or afterwards. Arsenal won 3-0 but it was the legendary Matthews, rather than our goals, which stuck in my memory."

The 1960s were not, as Anderson muses, a great time to be growing up an Arsenal supporter. The team were not particularly enterprising or successful and, to make it worse, other London sides, including the lot down the road were doing far better.

"Old men might go on about how dominant the club had been in the 1930s, but in the Sixties, with football in Britain on the up and up, Arsenal seemed to be on a downer and downer."

Even as England gloriously conquered the world on home soil in 1966, his team only contributed the elegant George Eastham to the squad, but he was never called upon to be in the team. *"Manchester United had George Best, Denis Law and Bobby Charlton. We had Ian bloody Ure!"*

Anderson recalls the other top teams' fans sang "You'll Never Walk Alone" and other rousing lyrics, whilst the Arsenal club chant appeared to be *"Billy Wright Must Go"*. Billy Wright was the David Beckham of his day – married to a pop star and everything – a player who'd had a glorious playing career and later did well in the media, but unfortunately, he failed as an Arsenal manager.

"I may have dreamt this, but I think at one poorly-attended evening match, a worried fan, fearing the never to be experienced relegation, took out a bugle and played the Last Post."

Things began to improve when Wright was finally shown the door and Arsenal promoted their club physio, Bertie Mee, to be the new manager. Anderson jokingly observes; *"It shows why Chelsea should have appointed Eva Carneiro as manager when they got rid of Jose Mourinho."*

In 1968 Arsenal finally had the chance to win the long-awaited trophy in the League Cup Final at Wembley, only to go behind to Don Revie's Leeds, who scored early, then wasted time cynically for the rest of the match.

"Could a trip to Wembley get any worse? Obviously it could, as the following year we contrived to lose to Swindon on the worst pitch

Wembley had ever produced. The game ended 3-1 after extra time and, even worse for me, I saw it from the Swindon end. It has psychologically damaged me for trips to Wembley ever since."

MISSED THEM ALL

In 1971, Wembley again threatened another disaster as Arsenal went behind to Liverpool in extra time, but; *"we managed a winner at the death. I say we managed – Charlie George did most of it – but you know what I mean."*

When Arsenal clinched the Double, it seemed things could only get better but, of course, this was Arsenal, and for most of the rest of the 1970s, things got worse and worse – until 1979.

Anderson contrived to miss one of the greatest moments as his team stole the long-awaited league title from Liverpool in the last minute at Anfield on the 26th May 1989. He spent the day making a short film in Brixton and was assured he would be finished by 5 pm at the latest, thus giving him plenty of time, not to get the match in Liverpool, but to get to a television set, quite possibly, at home.

In the event, the filming was not finished until 1am the next morning. The guy driving Anderson home, along with millions of other football fans, had seen it live on the telly, which was something of a rarity for a league game in those days.

"I am an Arsenal fan. Is it worth my while watching the match when I get in?" I asked him. He gave nothing away. "Well, I suppose you could watch it, if you want," he deadpanned. He must be great at poker, as nothing in his words, body language or driving gave anything away about how exciting the match had been as we chatted about other things all the way home."

So, everything was set for Anderson to experience the extraordinary nature of Michael Thomas' last gasp title clincher, only a few hours after everyone else... But...

"I was living in Islington, and as we got to the Angel, there were half-naked men dancing in the streets and red and white scarves were everywhere. Conga lines of fans... they certainly weren't there to offer goodhearted sporting congratulations to Liverpool, that's for sure!"

Work also forced Anderson to miss the climax of Wenger's first Double in 1998 because he was in LA recording a series of *Whose Line is it Anyway?* *"I think the dates were especially arranged by my producer, a Manchester United fan. I watched the vital match against Everton*

photo courtesy of Stuart Macfarlane and Arsenal FC

Anderson still misses Highbury... as do many Arsenal fans

and the Cup Final against Newcastle in a crowded British themed pub in Malibu, which sounds exotic, but it was a shame not to be closer to the action."

THEN AND NOW

So, being hugely successful and in demand, has certainly cost Anderson in terms of being as regular as he would have liked. Now things are less hectic, Anderson rarely misses a game, but in many ways, he misses the Highbury of his youth. As a teenager he would often stand at the Clock End in more innocent times before fans were so strictly segregated. Later, in his 20s, he and his friends would congregate in a favourite spot on the North Bank.

"Facilities for the ordinary fan on the terraces were pretty basic, but it was great to be able to just rock up to almost any game with anyone who wanted to go. Forward planning was not required. Season tickets, or buying any sort of tickets in advance, was only required for the posh seats."

Anderson now has a 'posh season ticket' himself, as he describes it; he does not however, think of himself as a posh fan. He lives close to the old ground and even closer to the new one. He appreciates the club moving grounds to make it slightly easier for him in his advancing years!

"I don't count myself as one of the prawn sandwich brigade as we eat at home before setting off for the match. Eating inside the stadium can cost an arm and a leg. Given the tickets to get in cost the other arm and leg, this is a useful economy measure."

INTERVIEWING AND MEETING A FEW HEROES

For folk of my age Clive Anderson was not only a trailblazer for his comedy shows but equally for his style of chat show. His offered a welcome break from the formulaic Wogan, Aspel or even Parkinson. He was cheeky, smart and risqué and his breaking of the mould opened the door for the likes of Jonathan Ross and Graham Norton to jump though and prosper.

I wondered if he recalled any opportunities his job had given him to mix work with pleasure and interview anyone connected to the Arsenal.

Whilst not claiming any credit, Anderson suggests that when Ian Wright was a guest on his show, it was one of the striker's first television appearances. Someone at the club had told him that Wright was brilliant at dealing with the media. He was indeed a superb guest with natural charisma and star quality. Of course his media career did indeed take off and, only a few years after retiring from football, Wright had his own Friday night chat show.

Around the same time Anderson had George Graham on as a guest promoting his book, *The Glory and the Grief*. The book included Graham's version of the financial irregularities which caused him to lose the Arsenal manager's role.

"I was determined to tease him about the topic, but he gave as good as he got – although he was punished eventually by being made to manage Spurs. I think he even won a trophy at White Hart Lane, so he must be good!"

Anderson has been fortunate to introduce, and to interview, Arsene Wenger at several Arsenal related events, but confesses he is no closer to understanding what makes the Frenchman tick.

"I would like to say I have gained a deep insight into what makes him tick, but he plays his cards pretty close to his chest. He gives as little away about himself as he does of Arsenal's money during the transfer

photo courtesy of Stuart Macfarlane and Arsenal FC

Anderson shares a joke with Arsene Wenger

window. Once I sat next to him at a pre-season dinner, hanging on his every word, without getting even a hint that Patrick Vieira was about to leave the club – which he did a week later."

CLIVE'S TEAM

Picking an all-time favourite Arsenal team is obviously almost impossible, but Anderson elected to give it a go:

In goal would be Pat Jennings. A marvellous keeper and according to Anderson a charming and modest man who once told him that, had he not made it as a footballer, would have worked on a building site.

"He had ludicrously large hands and lusciously thick hair before David Seaman. And of course the added bonus that he was snaffled from Spurs."

"In defence there are plenty to choose from, but we could have two Double-winning captains Tony Adams and Frank McLintock... Lee Dixon was an obvious and popular choice at right back. Less popular, but even more obvious at left-back, would be Ashley Cole, who had years playing at world class level at Arsenal and afterwards. But I am already worrying about leaving out David O'Leary, Sol Campbell and Kenny Sansom!"

In midfield Anderson elects to play Vieira in a defensive role. Many would debate this, but the rest of the team is so joyously attacking I am not sure it matters. As he says *"my general preference is for four across the back and all players ahead of that playing in a very fluid formation."*

"Up front I certainly want Dennis Bergkamp and Thierry Henry. In midfield you can't leave out Liam Brady. For attacking flair from mid-field I will go for Freddie Ljungberg and Robert Pires"

Balanced it may not be but with big Pat in between the sticks and a back four like that — but it is a formidable eleven. He says Paddy would be sitting in front of the back four with Bobby and Freddie either side of Liam, with Dennis and Thierry up top. For Anderson that is a 4-1-3-2 formation, transforming into more of a 4-4-2, or even 4-5-1, if forced into defence.

EPITAPH

I asked if Anderson recalled what he once said was his most over-used phrase and he did. For many of us long sufferers, through good and bad, it may not surprise you to learn that his given answer is *'Come on Arsenal!'*

I think I will conclude by again pinching how he would like to be remembered from the same Guardian interview with which I started...

"As a man who stayed hale and hearty until Arsenal won the Champions League in the year he was over 100 years old."

When this book comes out Anderson will be approaching 64 years of age, so with all due respect, Clive, I am not sure we all want to wait another 36 years until you get your Royal telegram for Arsenal's night of European glory.

So, come on Arsenal!

BIRDS OF A FEATHER... GUNNERS TOGETHER

There are two facets of comedy that the British particularly take to their hearts: one is a 'Double Act' and the other is of course the 'situation comedy'. Football itself has given us some fabulous double acts in recent times. The 1990s and early 2000s gave us Evans and Thompson, Evans and Houllier and lastly Houllier and Thompson. Whilst in and out of the act it was Thompson's presence that produced the show's famous catchphrase, 'Sit down Pinocchio!' A particular favourite double act of Arsenal fans is 'Lewis and Levy', who have been performing together for 15 years now at a small North London Comedy Club. Despite awful ratings and consistently poor reviews, for some reason this twosome have kept Gunners in tears of laughter. I guess it's all about personal taste when it comes to humour!

In all seriousness now, a phrase you will not read too often in this book – some of this country's finest comedy double acts are not those in front of the camera but those behind the typewriter. When I think of the collaborative writers of sit-coms in my lifetime three come to mind instantly – Croft and Perry, Le Frenais and Clement and of course Laurence Marks and Maurice Gran. Both were born in North London within earshot of Highbury. Marks and Gran have been creating hit comedy shows for nearly 50 years, and with the huge revival success of *Birds of a Feather,* show no signs of stopping. From *Holding the Fort* and *Shine on Harvey Moon* in the early 1980s through to *Birds of a Feather* in the later 80s and most of the 1990s, original and often cutting edge comedy produced by the writing combo was rarely absent from our televisions.

For me, however, it is for the creation of the perfect role for the late Rik Mayall as Alan B'Stard in the *New Statesman* that they will forever have my gratitude. Perfectly capturing the lack of compassion and the excesses of Thatcherism, with the assistance of an actor made for the role, Marks and Gran delivered so much more than a sitcom.

To have survived as a double-act for so long, I guessed there must be a fantastic chemistry between the two and I was not disappointed. Like an old married couple (and I mean that in the nicest way possible!) they interrupted each other, finished each other's sentences and complimented and prompted each other continually. What followed, for me, was two hours of stories and anecdotes from over 60 years of supporting The Arsenal, told with such warmth and rich humour. I departed laughing and smiled for two hours driving home relishing the task of selecting from an array of gems, whilst fearing I would not do them justice. I hope I have.

SEPARATE BOYHOOD JOURNEYS TO ARSENAL

The writing duo first met as new recruits to the Finsbury Park Company of the Jewish Boys Brigade in 1960. They played football together there, and elsewhere, all through the 60s, but their respective journeys into Arsenal support had begun earlier and were markedly different. What is crucial to them both, and comes across loud and clear, is that they supported their local team, even if Gran was a tad confused about that concept early on, as we will learn.

Laurence Marks' father started going just after we moved to Highbury after WW1. His brother, who is much older, started going in the Forties and carried on right through until about 1975, when his father died. Lawrence was first taken to Highbury himself as a four year old in 1953.

"I was tricked into going to the Arsenal. My father had a sweet shop in Hackney, and the bloke in the car dealer's next door told me one day we were all going to look at some cars, but they actually took me to the Arsenal as a surprise. I remember seeing Alex Forbes and Wally Barns."

"What struck me was this palace; I had never been anywhere, or seen anything, as big as Highbury. The green of the grass, I loved it. My dad asked me if I had enjoyed it and I said 'yes I really did' – I was only four – but I went to all the games thereafter."

Of course they were different times and from that first outing, once it was established that Marks was hooked, until he was about nine, he used to stand on a little stool that his dad had built him. They would get into the North Bank and his father would take him down to the front stand him on his stool and just ask the chaps standing around him to look out for his son, whilst he wandered off into the middle of the terrace where he liked to stand with Marks' older brother. It is hard to imagine a parent leaving his son in the company of strangers at four-years-old today but then it was considered safe. Although, one day…

"Arsenal used to have a forward with a ferocious shot called Cliff Holton, he burst through the middle and took this shot, which went flying past the post just over my head and hit the bloke behind me square in the chops and sent him flying."

In a sense the next 17 years were like a sentence because Arsenal were largely awful, whilst their arch rivals Spurs were largely very good – oh how times have changed! He jokes that he got to see so many great players, but sadly, very few in the red and white of his own team. He had to wait over ten years to start seeing competitive football and a flair player for Arsenal.

"I saw some of the best players and I don't mean for Arsenal. I never saw a really good player for my own team until Charlie George came along. I am not saying we'd not had the odd good player, of course we had, but never one with such flair."

Not unusually for those days, as we have heard from others, Marks would go to Arsenal one week and Tottenham the next. Unthinkable today, but most of his school friends were Spurs fans and even in 1960/61, when they did the Double, he went to virtually every game and his friends would then come to Highbury with him.

"There was intensity in the rivalry, but not the hatred in those days. In truth, there was no point because they were so much better than us."

Because Spurs were so good, even though he went to Holloway County School which was firmly in Arsenal territory, so many impressionable teenagers succumbed to the charms of the fantastic Tottenham side. Marks' school may ring a bell with many as it was a feeder school for the Arsenal and a young Laurence, for a time, played in the same team as Charlie George. It was a brief spell as George, his talent obvious to all, was soon put up an age group. He was briefly taught Maths and PE there by Bob Wilson, who was at Arsenal as an amateur initially, taught during the day.

Marks was born into a family where Arsenal was like a religion, and yet for so many years, he did not truly understand what it was like to see his team win with any regularity, let alone challenge. The recent nine years seems a short interlude by comparison. This was made harder by his father who would always tell stories of the wonderful Chapman side of the 1930s. He would wax lyrical to Laurence about the likes of Drake, Compton and James, but they were all just names to Marks. What did this greatness actually look like and would he ever see it at Highbury again?

"Then I saw Real Madrid in a friendly at Arsenal in a centenary game, but more importantly, in the 1960 European Cup Final at Hampden – they were simply the best team I had ever seen. I said to my Dad; 'Were Arsenal better than that?' And he said yes."

One of the greatest occasions Marks has ever witnessed was, ironically, a defeat – but it was more the momentous nature of the match and what it subsequently came to signify.

"I remember very clearly the match against Manchester United, which was their last game in England before the Munich disaster in which most of them lost their lives. (He showed me the programme) It was such a fantastic game. We went three down at half time against this truly fabulous team and brought it back to three all in about ten minutes in the second half. It ended 5-4 to them, but it was just a privilege to have been there."

The date was the 12 February 1958, the Manchester United team were the Busby Babes, and as Marks points out, it was to be their last match on English soil before they flew to Yugoslavia to play Red Star Belgrade. Eight of that team, who had won successive titles, would not return from the trip, dying in the tragic Munich air disaster. Marks did get to see such greatness again in N5, but he had to wait a fair few more years to do so... But more of that later.

So, what of his partner Maurice Gran, was he too born into the Arsenal? Well the answer is firmly not. Gran's father was not really a football man, and when asked who he supported, he would say 'eight draws!' In fact, so alien to the young Gran was the concept of being a football fan and supporting his local team that he did not realise there was one. It is ironic today as he is fiercely passionate of the concept, but as a young lad....

"We lived in Finsbury Park Road, on one of the roads where people used to park their cars on a match day. I didn't really understand why once every two weeks or so the road would suddenly fill up with cars or what those strange lowing noises I could hear on a Saturday afternoon were!"

Gran thinks the first game he remembers consciously was the 1957 Cup Final between Manchester United and Aston Villa, aged seven. He didn't really understand it, but he knew he wanted to. In the same way as he liked playing football in the playground, whilst not really comprehending the finer points of the game.

"It was around that time that one of my father's friends asked me, when we were on holiday in Margate, which football team I supported? For some reason I said Queens Park Rangers. So he said 'why do you support QPR?' I told him I liked the name, which I did, when they read the results out. Even though they were in the Third Division. He said 'why would you support them when you live round the corner from The Arsenal?' To which I replied 'do I?'"

Gran had lived within a mile of Highbury without realising that was the case, but once he did know, he declared Arsenal as his team and began pestering his uncle to take him. He promised to take his nephew once Maurice could convince him he knew all the players and positions.

As Gran recalled, this must have taken him over two years, or his uncle could not get the tickets, because it look that long from his realisation that he had a local team to support and he eventually got to see them live.

The match in question, in December 1959, was at home to Burnley, who went on to become Champions. Arsenal were 2-0 up at half-time and went on to lose 4-2, which as Gran says, encapsulated the Arsenal of that time quite well. No matter however, as he was smitten, and over the next few years, his uncle would take him occasionally and they would always sit in the Upper Tier.

Once in senior school, William Ellis, where unlike at Holloway County, most of Gran's compatriots were Gunners, he began to go on his own. This was when the club developed a school boys' enclosure at the front of the Lower East Stand. With a family not instantly inclined to encourage his growing habit, and too young to be working, Gran revealed a novel way to secure the funds to see his newly beloved team.

"Once, when I was about 13, I managed to get to an Everton game midweek by way of putting my mother's groceries on the slate for about three weeks leading up the game. She would send me around the corner with coins to buy her things, but I would tell the shopkeeper my mother had asked me if she could put in on the slate." Marks and I suggest his poor mother must have realised at some point

"Well, she wasn't a very good manager of money. I did do naughty things to see the team, but on that occasion, it was well worth it as we won 4-3." (26 March 1963)

Whilst still laughing at the image of Gran, the mischievous little scamp, defrauding his own mother to see the Arsenal and being liberal with the truth with his kindly local grocer, he went on to shatter any sympathy we may have had for the shopkeeper he conned...

"The shop with the slate was run by a chap who was a dyed in the wool Tottenham supporter. It was just round the corner from us in Blackstock Road. If I went in there to ask for anything or, to put groceries on the slate, he would demand, 'only if you say 'Spurs are better than Arsenal' three times out loud' or something similar. He was a total wind up merchant."

Not having the father to take him and pay for him, like Marks had, he was often working at the weekend and it was not until the mid-1970s that Gran was able to go to Arsenal with regularity, by which stage the pair were writing partners – they have been going together ever since.

NOT BEING AT LIVERPOOL IN 1989

After a pretty awful time in the early 1980s Arsenal had returned to winning ways in 1987, defeating the old enemy in the Littlewood Cup Semi Final, and Liverpool in the Final. Gran recalls the fabulous second replay at White Hart Lane with some glee….

"We went to the replay at Spurs, the one nil down two one up semi replay. The reason it's so sacred in my memory and that of all those who were there, on about 88 minutes Spurs were still winning and they chose to announce the arrangements for their prematurely-celebrating fans, to get their tickets for the final. That's why, in my mind, that turn around was so delicious."

It was the start of a fabulous period in the early George Graham era, although back then it was the dawn of the fanzine, and like the bloggers of today, as Gran recalls, they always thought they knew better than the boss. Marks and Gran would always stop and buy *1 Nil Down 2 One Up* from its founder Tony Willis on the way to the ground.

"We always used to buy the fanzine from him on our way into Highbury during the George Graham era. I remember Willis saying 'we all know we need a centre forward and what does he do? He buys a centre forward from a poor side who are about to be relegated and then he lends him back to them. I don't know, seems mad to me!'"

It was the same centre forward the following season, Smudger Smith, who won the Golden Boot and sent the team on its way to the memorable 2-0 victory requited at Anfield on the 26 May 1989. Neither of the pals was at the match, but both recall the night well.

Marks' wife was working on Shakespeare in the Park, so she was out that evening, and he had invited a friend (who shall remain nameless) round to watch the match. Of course Nick Hornby's book and film, *Fever Pitch*, portrayed the story as well as anyone, but Marks' evening of two nervous friends watching from the sofa has a slightly different ending. It seems Marks' companion was more nervous than most Gunners who were perhaps resigned to disappointment.

"He was continually knocking back vodka and blackcurrant juices during the game. So it was one nil, he was still drinking and then when Thomas scored that second with a minute to go he just vomited red and white all over my sofa, on the carpet and everywhere."

"So there was red and white vomit on that celebratory night which I had to do my best to clean up before my wife arrived home. But she did tell me that when Arsenal scored the goal that won the title the audience just began spontaneously cheering in Regents Park, during Midsummer Night's Dream. So I can confirm that Arsenal and Michael Thomas interrupted Shakespeare."

OUR FRIEND MELVYN WHO OCCASIONALLY BRAGGS

Marks and Gran are modest chaps, and in 1991, at the absolute peak of their success with the *New Statesman*, they'd not really mentioned what they did to those who sat around them week in week out at Highbury. The same could not be said of their near neighbour in the ground, Melvyn Bragg, who sat with his son Tom. You know how it is at football, you often chat to those around you, but although Melvyn knew their names, he did not know what they did. Ironic really, as he was the front man of the foremost Arts programme on television, *The South Bank Show*.

Arsenal were closing in on their second title in two seasons and were playing at home to Leeds United, which the Gunners won 2-0, with both goals by Kevin Campbell in the last 15 minutes. Melvyn Bragg, however, missed both the goals as he left with 20 minutes to go. He had been telling those around him that he had to leave early that day because he had to get home and changed to be at the BAFTAs at The Grosvenor House, where in the Best Cultural Documentary category, his show filled all five nominations. Maurice's dry response at the time was *'I expect you are going to win then Melvyn.'*

"We didn't say anything and left at the normal time and then of course we went to the BAFTAs too. We had been nominated for 'Best Comedy' for the New Statesman. So, after the awards, Melvyn was at the after party, which is always shit, holding his BAFTA and we walked up to him holding our BAFTA and said 'are you going to the game next week?' and his jaw dropped. It was so funny. 'Why didn't you say anything?' he asked and I said; 'Well, unlike you, we did not know we were going to win!' "

Long after Marks and Gran had given up those particular seats, they were reconnected with Melvyn, when, in 1997, he made a *South Bank Show* about them! Getting to know them better Bragg invited them to join a group of friends including writers, lawyers and publicists who used to meet for lunch, or occasionally dinner, before or after Arsenal matches. The highbrow group called itself the 'Crescit Club' and would meet at San Daniele Restaurant in Highbury Park to put right the wrongs of team selection, tactics and club policy – a bit like an upmarket version of The Tollington or Twitter today by the sounds of it!

Gran recalls it became quite the place to be seen and many of the players in the early Wenger era, particularly the overseas ones, would come there after the game. He remembers Patrick Viera being kept waiting outside in his tracksuit until a table came free on one occasion.

INVESTING IN THE CLUB WE LOVED

The pair went to watch Arsenal in Turin when they won the Cup Winners Cup in 1994, where they were hanging out with the press boys, and in particular, Harry Harris. In 1994 Harris was on the top of his game; Sports Journalist of the Year, Chief Football writer at the Mirror. They told Harris, who was close to the club, that they were keen to use their writing talents to contribute to the Arsenal. They suggested a magazine or fanzine because they felt the programme was too boring. Harris immediately offered to introduce them to David Dein at the earliest opportunity, not expecting this to be the same day, as Gran recalls.

"Later we were walking around the lovely shopping arcade in Turin, in a very fancy shop called Valentino's, we saw David Dein in the downstairs men's section because his wife was in the upstairs ladies bit. I thought 'David's thinking if we are in here much longer I am going to have to sell a player!"

Harry, good to his word, took them in and introduced them. He said something along the lines of *'David, this is Laurence Marks and Maurice Gran, huge Arsenal fans and they're really interested in talking to you about some ideas they have for the club. You might know them? They are television writers who have just sold their company for £46 million."*

Gran clearly remembers seeing a flicker going across David's face, perhaps concern? Actually what had happened was that the company that Marks and Gran's company was a small part of had been sold for £46 million and they only owned 5% of it.

"The reality was that we'd paid off our mortgages and had a few quid in the bank –but inadvertently a message had struck home with David Dein saying we had some interesting suggestions for the club, swiftly followed by the company sale line – Dein obviously thought 'Oh fuck these two are going to try and get on the board.'"

Marks suggested that they should all meet up for lunch back home at his club, The Reform. At this point Dein accepted gracefully, but asked if he could bring Danny Fiszman with. In hindsight, as Gran elaborates, *"Dein is obviously thinking these guys have got a lot of money and there could be trouble so I need Danny with me!"* Marks added,

"They obviously thought we wanted to buy the club or something, but all we wanted to do was start a new magazine with their blessing."

The boys only wish they had realised back then that Dein, courtesy of Harris's inadvertent introduction, had got the wrong signals because they really would have had some fun with that misconception. Reinforced with the main man Fiszman, Dein once settled at the table for lunch had nervously asked *'So chaps what is that really bothers you about the club then? 'To* which the boys had honestly replied *"We don't wish to cause offence but the Match Day Programme is really boring."*

 "You could literally see the colour return to Dein's face and Harry Harris said 'yes the guys are great writers and would like to start a magazine called the North Bank.'"

A relieved Dein and Fiszman proceeded to tell them that they were about to launch a new Arsenal Magazine, which was to be monthly, and called the *Gunners* and suggested that perhaps Marks and Gran might like to write a column for that. The partners happily agreed, so Dein asked what they would want in return, still seemingly thinking he could not afford them! After a short moment they replied; *"Two Season Tickets, a car parking place, lunch before the game and access to players please."*

Two very relieved Arsenal Directors were true to their word and Marks and Gran, for the next three years, had new season tickets, lunch in the Mezzanine and a car park pass. A small price to pay to stave off two likely lads who Dein thought had £46 million burning a hole in their pockets ready to shake up the club.

LAURENCE THE DIARIST

Laurence has always been a diarist and Maurice had suggested he should use his thoughts on Arsenal, recorded day to day, and then turn them into a book. The resulting 'Fan for all Seasons' - The Diary of an Arsenal Supporter' was published in early 2000 and covers Mark's musings from the start of 1996/97 to the end of 1998/99.

Marks referred to the book on a few occasions when we met, but along with dedications to Gran, the members of the Crescit Club, special thanks are reserved to David Dein, who became a friend after the earlier amusing misunderstanding and was exceedingly helpful in allowing him access to Colney, the Arsenal players and to Arsene Wenger.

Laurence Marks and David Dein at Babi Yar in Kiev

While he was writing the book, Marks had wanted to go through the final season keeping the diary, so for authenticity, he wanted to follow them home and away and in Europe. He thought the European experiences would be interesting chapters and it was in Kiev, in November 1998, that he properly renewed his acquaintance with David Dein. He was in the reception at the hotel feeling lost and a man had approached him asking if he was Jewish. When Marks had replied in the affirmative, the chap had asked if he would like to join him and his family and friends on a City tour, taking in the Caves Monastery and Babi Yar the next day. This generous spirited stranger was Arnold Dein and the party included his son and his younger brother, David, and his wife Barbara. In the end he joined them for a meal at the only Kosher restaurant in Kiev that night and on the sightseeing excursion. David and Arnold's father had been born in the City.

"David was lovely and, of course, remembered me from the infamous meetings in Turin and Reform and said to come to his hotel to meet Arsene. So, I told him about the book chronicling my year following Arsene Wenger's Arsenal, and he offered to help in any way he could."

Marks observes that Dein is a modest man with a superb sense of humour but, in truth, just appeared to be an Arsenal fan, living his dream and pinching himself daily, to be Vice-Chairman. Before Babi Yar they visited the Monastery Caves where in the 11th century, monks spreading the Christian word lived and worshipped, but are also buried. The combination of cool temperature and humid atmosphere apparently has caused the Monks bodies to mummify and they lie there almost perfectly preserved.

"As we walked around the caves David Dein stopped at one of the mummified bodies, wrapped in whatever mummified monks are usually wrapped in, turned to me and said 'Now I know what happened to Gus Caesar!"

Dein subsequently arranged for Marks to go to Colney and meet with Tony Adams and Arsene Wenger, and for his help, the book's main dedication was to him.

ARSENE WHO?

But back to where the book journey began, in the summer of 1996 and the dismissal of Bruce Rioch; the speculation as to why he was sacked and who might succeed him. In the preface Marks asked whether Gooners would have wanted a stalwart, unimaginative, English manager rather than an unknown foreigner called Arsene Wenger. Well, as Marks looked back to his diary entries in the summer of 1996, that did indeed seem to be the case.

Gran recalls a conversation with Harry Harris, as the amateur sleuths tried to get to the bottom of Rioch's sudden dismissal. Harris whispered that the story doing the rounds at Highbury, and in the press room, was that the departed manager was known as 'Dagenham' behind his back. When he had asked why, Harris had replied *"because he was two stops past Barking."*

Gran had continued his investigation on the first day of the season, and after parking up in the ground, he left Marks to go out and seek out his trusty source, Tony Willis, the editor of *1 Nil Down 2 One Up*, the alternative voice of the Arsenal faithful, to see if he had the inside track on the unknown Frenchman or a more serious candidate. Willis was unequivocal; *"Nah you don't want some foreigner from Japan who knows nothing about English Football, Frank Clark's available."* It is this anecdote that concludes the preface of the book.

The speculation was soon confirmed and Wenger would become the new manager but not until October. Marks and Gran recall being in the Mezzanine, when early that season, they were unwittingly introduced to two new Arsenal signings, Garde and Vieira. It was the beginning of the Wenger revolution even before he had been announced. Gran summarised his view at the time… they can't be proper footballers if they are French!

In the case of Patrick Vieira their doubts were swiftly dispelled as Marks recollects:

"Of course a month later we were there on a cold September evening to see Arsenal v Sheffield Wednesday and Vieira came on after about 20 minutes – I remember thinking I have just never seen a player like that in 40 years of watching football."

Wenger's first full season saw the Arsenal win a memorable League and FA Cup Double, 27 years after the last in 1971, but as the writing partner reflect what happened in the last few months of the campaign had not looked so likely in the winter of 1997.

As Marks recalls, Gran was something of a prophet (but not of doom) when all around him doubted the team. On the 13 December 1997, after two defeats and a narrow win over Newcastle, Blackburn had come to North London and given the Gunners a footballing lesson and had beaten them at Highbury.

So appalled at the display, they had left early and Marks suggested to Gran that the defeat had effectively ended Arsenal's title aspirations. The result left Arsenal in fifth, seven points behind the leaders Manchester United with a goal difference 19 worse off and having played a game more.

"Maurice said the oddest thing, especially for someone with so much common sense. 'You know, I think Arsenal will win the Double.' I said 'why?' and he replied 'because today will be the turning point.'"

Gran takes up the tale of his faith. He suggests that Tony Adams obviously agreed with him, because it was after that game that the skipper, so the story goes, turned to Petit and Viera and said we (the defence) can't do everything, we need protection.

"I had a strange feeling about it, so I went the bookies, and I am not a big betting man, but I put a tenner on us to win the Double at 20-1. If I won the bet I was going to treat myself to a shirt I had seen in Gieves and Hawkes on Sloane Square. It was the first floral shirt I had seen since about 1967 and it was fantastic. It was floral with while collar and cuffs and it was £125. That was an awful lot of money – I still have it to this day and it will always remind me of Wenger's first Double."

Gran's faith in his team was not, however, reflected in his faith in one of Wenger's newest signings that season, a certain young French-

man called Nicolas Anelka. He remembers being in the Directors Box for a terrible match at Stamford Bridge in the League Cup, when Arsenal played a weakened team and 'threw' the game. An angry Gran had turned to Dein and asked a question he had absolutely no right to ask, *"How can you bear to pay Anelka's wages? He didn't chase the ball, he just stands there sulking. What is he even doing on the pitch? David said 'the Manager says he won't learn in the reserves.'"*

Of course, about six weeks later, it all clicked. But Gran remembers Laurence asking him at about the same time why Anelka didn't chase the ball. He had replied, as a joke, *'What you've got to realise is he has such a finely tuned football brain that he can calculate the speed of the ball against his own speed and work out instantly whether it's worth chasing it. Only weeks later, when Wrighty was injured and Anelka was playing with Bergkamp and banging them in, someone asked Wenger why his young French striker sometime does not chase the ball down and he replied 'He knows exactly the speed of the ball and whether it is worth chasing!"*

MEETING WENGER

David Dein was as good as his word and arranged for Marks to meet with Wenger. He describes the great man as very funny, with a dry sense of humour. He asked the manager about the changes he made when he had first arrived at the club and what he'd been looking for when he first saw the players he had inherited in training. In response Wenger had offered to tell Marks a story. It went something like this...

Wenger – 'I was stood on the training ground watching from the side line as if I were Herbert von Karajan conducting the Berlin Philharmonic. I was watching with interest Mr Parlour and I said Mr Parlour could you just come over here please? So Mr Parlour came over to me.'

Parlour – 'What is it Boss?'

Wenger – 'Could you tell me why you are playing in the centre of midfield?'

Parlour – 'Well that is where I have always played. It's where Mr Graham used to play me. I am the fetcher and carrier boss.'

Wenger - 'But why, Mr Parlour?'

Parlour (Confused) – Like I said boss that is where Mr Graham played me and where I always play.'

AW – 'Yes, but why?'

Ray – 'What is it boss, aren't I doing it right or something?'

Wenger – 'Let me tell you something, Mr Parlour. When the ball comes to you from the right hand side and you are playing centre midfield it takes you (something like) 0.43 seconds to control the ball and move off. When it comes to you from the left you do it in half the time. So I suggest Mr Parlour you go and play on the right and you will play there for England within a year.'

Of course Parlour did move to the right, played in 47 of Arsenal's 52 matches in 1997/98, won the Double *and* was Man of the Match in the FA Cup Final. He also made the England preliminary squad for the 1998 World Cup only to be axed by Hoddle for the famous 'short back and sides' comment to Eileen Drewery.

Marks meeting the manager and skipper

BEING A GOONER, EVEN IF A TAD DISCONNECTED

Marks and Gran are still season ticket holders at the Emirates, but they don't feel the same connection with the new stadium as the old home. This, combined with television dominating football scheduling has, in a way, disconnected them to a large degree. It got to a point where they were not enjoying it enough to justify the travel and the inconvenience. As Gran says;

"I changed from being a person that found 'not going' was unimaginable, to a person who will now get a couple of mates round, get a few beers in and watch it on the telly. All down to Sky Sports and their crazy

kick off times. What's changed with football, and this is the triumph of Sky, is that 90% of football fans never even consider that going to the game is part of being a football fan. Being a fan is watching a game on TV, or at the pub, with your mates, with a shirt on."

Marks accepts that Arsenal did, what they had to do, in moving to the new stadium – but in the process – they disconnected with a lot of supporters. Even many of those that still go feel disconnected.

"The cost is ridiculous. We're alright, we can afford it, but if my dad was still alive today he would not have been able to take me to the Arsenal. We sat behind a bloke with his two sons and he was saying to us it was costing him about £300 or £400 for each game, and if there was another game in the week, say a European match, it could be £800 – he couldn't afford it. So who goes?"

Despite their current disaffection, the love of the club is, and always will be, close to their hearts and both reflect that where ever they have worked in the world, and for a long period living in America, there was never a week where the Arsenal result was not an important part of their day.

"You follow a club through adversity but why do you follow a club? What is a club? Is it a place? No. Is it a team? Obviously not! Is it a manager? No. Is it a shirt? No, well sometimes, but they fuck around with that. It's the memories isn't it, and it's the kids you went to school with, or your dad, or your uncle."

"Football turns us back into school boys and that is why we love it. Because you can drop everything and you can take it seriously because it is not important." What he means, of course, is it that it is massively important to each and every one of us that follows a team, but equally, you can argue vociferously about it without ever falling out, unlike over money or politics.

FINALLY DAD

An appropriate way to conclude with Marks and Gran was to bring it back to the young Laurence Marks being brought up on tales of the great Arsenal team of the 1930s and enduring 17 years of utter rubbish, whilst loving every minute. The second leg against Anderlecht in 1970, which ended the trophy drought, was the most special night at Highbury – but the final game of 2003/4, beating Leicester to finish the season undefeated, was the most memorable occasion and achievement.

"Arsenal fans can honestly say they have seen the best six years of football this country has ever produced. Manchester United for all that they achieved, never produced football like the magical football Wenger's Arsenal produced from 1998 to 2004. Those were the times my Dad was talking about in the 1930s."

ARSENAL TALES FROM THE AFTER DINNER CIRCUIT

Many of the Arsenal comedians in this book are household names, with the others falling into the category of 'should be' or 'will be'. When I asked Gary Marshall, the King of the Sportsman's Dinner, if he regrets that television seems to have passed him by, the answer is an unequivocal no. His feeling is that to make a living making people laugh is reward itself, but to make them laugh together with sporting greats is 'stealing a living really!'

Marshall has huge admiration for the modern day observational comedians, who continually challenge themselves, writing brand new material for new stand up shows. That is not the comedian that he wants, or claims to be. He is an old style gag teller, with skills honed on the Northern Working Men's Club circuit, with a relaxed, deadpan delivery and punchline timing of the highest order. As Matt Le Tissier, who often works with Marshall, said for his website; 'His timing and delivery is a work of art!' The man himself suggests a mentor once told him when starting out as a stand-up; it takes ten years of experimenting until you have truly matured, found your own style and what is right for you. "My style is the pause, before the deadpan punchline. I'm miserable, but not quite as miserable as Jack Dee."

This would be a wonderful example if it works in print...

"I think the best bit of advice I was ever given in life came from my Grandad. He said, 'son, you will never get anywhere in life without opening doors. That was quite profound for him. He's dead now obviously." (Deadpan expression and long pause) "He got sucked out of an aeroplane."

Gary's bedroom wall in around 1977

DONCASTER GUNNER

The clue above about a craft learned the hard way in Northern Working Men's clubs, suggests that this particular Gunner does not hail from North London. In fact Marshall is a 'Donnie' lad – born, raised and still living with his own family in Doncaster. Add into the melting pot that his whole family were die hard Manchester United fans, it does beg the question, why Arsenal?

As we will learn, through his profession, Marshall has been fortunate enough to have met and worked with many Arsenal greats, but sadly he has not yet met the one who started it all for him aged six.

"The man I have not met, and a player who I would love to meet is John Radford – he's why I am an Arsenal fan. It was the 1971 Cup Final. I was 6, stopping at my Nan's house, and I had never seen a game of football in my life. So, I put the TV on expecting the Banana Splits but instead it was the build up to the FA Cup Final. When I switched on John Radford was talking in a broad Yorkshire accent and I thought 'I'll have these'."

In truth, he had no idea who Arsenal were, or where the club was, but from that day, 8 May 1971, Arsenal were his team. Obviously when they won the match the deal was clinched and, much to his family's annoyance, he has been Arsenal for life. Marshall admits now that his own children were given no choice, they were Gunners at birth, but back in 1971 his family thought it was just a child's whim.

"My family thought I was mad, living in Doncaster, it was pointless for years. I did not meet another Arsenal fan in Doncaster until I was about 20. Now there are about 12 of us!"

His first experience of watching his beloved Arsenal in the flesh came in May 1977 when one of his Dad's friends, who was connected, took him to see them at Old Trafford. Better still he was able to take the excited 12 year old Gary into the Player's Lounge after the game. He already had a bedroom plastered with Shoot magazine pictures of his heroes, but as with many young fans, that season his hero was Arsenal's record breaking £333,333 signing, Malcolm Macdonald. The Gunners beat a very accomplished United side that, a few weeks later, would lift the FA Cup, and Marshall recalls Brady and Stapleton, two more of his idols, scored.

BEDROOM WALL CIRCA 1977

Could the day get any better for the star-struck lad as he entered the Player's Lounge programme and pen at the ready? Would he really get to meet his bandy-legged super-striking hero? To the young Marshall's distress, despite getting a few top autographs, Macdonald was nowhere to be seen in the lounge. Someone told his Dad's friend that the man he sought was elsewhere.

"He was in outside in the car park smoking a fag. He put it out and walked straight past me without a glance. He was about 30 yards in front of me by the time I plucked up the courage, not wanting to miss the opportunity. I was a 12 year old kid, in a horrendous purple trench coat my dad had bought me and I squeaked 'Supermac' and he turned round and went 'Fuck off kid.' I met him recently as an adult at a do and was tempted to go up to him and say 'Remember me Supemac?' in a high pitched voice."

They do say 'never meet your heroes', but when it comes to Arsenal, 'Supermac' is on his own as a disappointment in a very long list of Gunner legends Marshall has met and worked alongside. More of that shortly, but first back to Doncaster 1979 and the FA Cup final in a household with one teenage Gunner surrounded by Yorkshire Reds.

Marshall recalls the day vividly. Arsenal were two to the good at half time and the young Marshall was on cloud nine. Even more so when his best mate, a Leeds fan, turned up at the break; an ally with whom he could enjoy the misery his team were inflicting on the rest of his household.

"Then Gordon McQueen and Sammy McIlroy scored and I can remember I left the lounge through this big archway we had and I was on the stairs nearly crying at 2-2. But then came my Fever Pitch moment, even before Fever Pitch, if you know what I mean? My Dad shouted 'quick lad' and I ran through the archway just as Brady passed to Rix who crossed beautifully for Sunderland to score the winner. Then I was punching the archway in happiness."

FELL INTO STAND UP

Of course it was eight years later, when Marshall was into his 20s and had found the other 11 Gunners in Doncaster, that Arsenal were to win again. By then the rebellious teenager was a full-time comedian, a career path that was far from planned. After leaving school he worked for a Ladbrokes Bingo, initially as a caller, and later as a trainee manager, before getting the sack. He had no trade as such so his dad, who used to be comedian, pulled a few strings and got him a job as a Butlin's Red coat at the Metropole Hotel Blackpool, for the last few months of the season. In the first week his manager called him in, told him there was a show on the Thursday, and he wanted Gary to do a 20-minute slot. When the newest Red Coat enquired '20 minutes of what?' the answer was '20 minutes of comedy of course'. The assumption had been made that because his dad was a comic, the young ex-bingo caller would be too. When Marshall protested that he had never told a gag in anger the response was along the lines of 'oh well, we have not got a comic for the show so give it a go and help us out.'

"So my dad wrote me a little script, which I sort of learned in two days. I came on with a little bit of paper with the bullet points on to remind me and stuck it on the microphone stand and went from there really. It went great, but it gives you a false sense of security. You are with these people all week, looking after them and they are willing you to do well."

Nevertheless after two successful seasons making a supportive audience laugh, Marshall decided he was ready for the tough, 'real world' comedy circuit. It had become his calling and, in a move that can only be seen as ironic, as Maggie Thatcher destroyed the mining communities all around his Doncaster home, the Tories gave Marshall a leg up. Whilst many he knew were having their careers threatened and their livelihood ripped away, the same government introduced 'The Youth Opportunities Training Scheme', in 1987.

"I thought I'll have a go at this. If you stuck £2,000 in your bank they would pay you £40 a week for a year to start a new business. So the business was Gary Marshall Comedian."

As Marshall worked hard in the pubs and clubs in the late Eighties and early Nineties, his Arsenal support stayed firm and he and a few of the other 'Donnie Gooners' became active members of the Yorkshire Arsenal Supporters Club.

"They were the most boring set of bastards you will ever meet in your life. They would not let you have a drink on the coach. Ridiculous trips – it used to start in Leeds and then come to Doncaster and then go via bloody Cambridge, miles out of the way, to pick up the Chairman, Andy Hill, who had lived in Leeds but had moved there. You would set off at crazy o'clock and they would put some totally inappropriate film on like The Matrix. 'Why the fuck are we watching The Matrix? Put some bloody comedy on that we can dip in and out of, not the bloody Matrix'. They also used to make us leave the match about five minutes early so the coach could beat the traffic. Like when we won the title in '98. You would want to stay and celebrate wouldn't you? Oh no, not that lot! They were the weirdest bunch of people. So we packed that in."

So where do his tickets come from now? Funny you should ask...

MY FRIEND DAVID

Marshall first met David Dein at a Royal Variety Club Golf Society Stag do at which Dein had taken a table. The annual bash is one of the biggest nights on the circuit and Marshall has been lucky to be asked to be on the top table twice. The audience is over 800 strong and a huge number of them are from the world of entertainment and sport. In December 2006, on the first occasion, the Top Table boasted the likes of Pat Jennings, Russ Abbott, Jasper Carrot, John Conteh and other massive names. Marshall was in esteemed company and knew it was the biggest gig he had ever done. He recalls the nerves well and then he also spied opportunity knocking...

"I was thinking if I die on my arse here word is going to get around the business so quickly. I spotted David Dein on the front table and then I got thinking, hello Gary lad, if you do well here you could be in at Arsenal. I had gone down on my own and I rang the Mrs and said David Dein is right here in front of me, if I nail it here you never know."

Marshall delivers a gag for his tickets

As it transpired he delivered a great set and he had 700 of the 800 up on their feet giving him a standing ovation. He was on such a high he momentarily forgot about David Dein and the fact that Liam Brady was on his table – he went straight outside to ring his wife and share his joy. As he was telling his wife that it has been the best night of his career, and wondering if he had the balls to go back in and introduce himself to David and Liam, he saw Dein stride past to the cloakroom and retrieve his coat and scarf. There was still a huge charity auction to come, but the Arsenal Vice-Chairman was clearly a busy man and not staying. For Marshall it was then or never...

"Mr Dein, excuse me, and he turned around and said; 'lovely set young man'. I said 'thank you Sir I am a massive Arsenal fan'. 'Are you really?' I said 'anything I can do at Arsenal or for the club...' He gave me his card and he said; 'Gary we would love to use you.' I have his card I have his word."

It took Marshall a few months to pluck up the courage to use the card and the number on it to ask Dein for tickets, but the Arsenal Vice Chairman was gracious on the phone and good to his word. But then...

"I would say six days later, we were driving somewhere and Ian Wright was on Talksport and it came on the news that Dein had gone. I couldn't believe it; I had waited all my professional life for a break like that and to get a foot in at Arsenal and that happened."

Thankfully, for Marshall, whilst his esteemed new contact had never been able to employ him for work at the club, he has always been true to his word when it comes to match tickets. Dein has 14 of 16 Club Level seats and has always come good for one or two, as long as Marshall gives him enough notice. However, whilst the great man has never allowed the Yorkshire funny man to pay, there has always been a particular price put on the tickets. Dein clearly enjoys a good joke and probably uses them on his guests – the condition for Marshall's tickets is always to have a new gag or two before they are handed over.

Often Marshall, having partaken of a 'few tinnies' on the train down from Doncaster, is not in the best state to deliver his finest gag, but Dein always insists and he always laughs graciously and hands over the match tickets. Sometimes it is David's son Gavin, or even another friend, but the ritual of the joke telling before handover is observed.

"It must be the weirdest thing for other fans and families walking past seeing me, a large spikey haired Yorkshire man telling gags to David Dein outside the Emirates."

TALES FROM THE AFTER DINNER CIRCUIT

A huge amount of Marshall's work is at the Sportsman's Dinner and testimonial circuit and, consequently, he is usually one of two after dinner speakers. The sports person and comedian double act is perfect for such events – there are many regulars who enjoy delivering the after dinner speech on a Q&A and Marshall gets on with nearly all of them. Some, like Jan Molby and Matt Le Tissier, he is particularly fond of and the man he admired the most, certainly as an inspirational speaker, was former Arsenal skipper and World Cup winner Alan Ball. He has worked with 1971 heroes Frank McLintock, Eddie Kelly and Bob Wilson, all of whom he considers to be true gentlemen of the Arsenal. However, when it comes to the Gooners, Paul Merson and Ray Parlour are in a league of their own.

Paul Merson has always been very honest about his issues in the past with drugs, drink and his gambling addiction. There are a few stories in Merson's own excellent book; but no harm in relaying a few of Marshall's personal favourites from The Magic Man's after dinner sessions. The first thing Marshall wants to stress though, is that whilst Merson is a Chelsea fan, he always wants the team that made him, Arsenal, to do well, and contrary to popular belief, Wenger did not want to sell him – he wanted to go.

M AND M

Marshall recalls that when Merson began doing these events he preferred a Q&A style for 45 minutes, then he would follow him . They worked this routine on four or five occasions and then one day, at a restaurant in Manchester, Merson turned up and declared he had written a script and learned it. Marshall expressed his surprise at the time, but then Merse stood up and delivered a faultless 50-minute performance with some cracking tales within it. A favourite of Marshall's from the Merson repertoire, which he does not use any more, concerned his skipper Tony Adams.

Cast your mind back to the title run in in 1989 and you may recall an unusual away draw at Old Trafford. Arsenal had gone behind but pulled it back to 1-1 with both goals from Merse's skipper and mentor Tony Adams. On the coach home Adams had a quiet word with Merse, asking if he could crash at his place as he was having a few issues at home. Merse called his wife to give her advanced warning before they all got back to London and went to the pub where they had a lock-in until two in the morning. The pair arrived back at the two-up-two-down the young striker had back then and Adams was put up on a new sofa bed in the lounge.

Remarkable as it may seem now, the lovely British tabloids had not yet warmed to Arsenal's on-pitch leader, perhaps after the torrid time he had in the Euros the previous summer. The next morning Merse was up early and out to get the newspaper from the local garage while Adams was still sleeping it off. He was shocked to see the back pages hammering his skipper, friend and current house guest, calling him 'Donkey Adams' and worse. For Merse that was totally over the top but he certainly didn't have the heart to let Adams see it. Marshall recounts the tale as Merse told it...

'It will kill him if he saw this!' So he got back to the house, hiding the papers and asked Tony if he wanted any breakfast. Adams politely declined the offer, just tea for him and then he would get off. So Merse makes the tea, keeping the papers out of sight. Merse was proud to have protected his skipper from the hateful headlines and was relieved when Adams left the house. He watched from the kitchen window and just as Adams was closing the gate, Merse caught the awful scent of something he recognised wafting from his new sofa bed.

"He'd pissed himself on my new sofa bed! So I chased him down the road shouting 'you pissed on my bloody sofa bed you fucking donkey!'"

Marshall probably works more with Merse [pictured above] than anyone and they are a popular double act on the circuit, but he is still continually surprised by the former Gunner's compulsive and continual gambling. To illustrate the point he describes an afternoon and evening in Penrith with Merse.

As soon as they met up the first questions was whether Marshall has had a bet that afternoon.

Merse – "You have a bet Gaz?"

Marshall – "Yes I have a had a small one Merse."

Merse – "What you on?"

Marshall – "I have had Wigan plus six versus Leeds in the Rugby League."

Merse – "Why have you done that?"

Marshall –"Well I just fancy them mate. They have just run into a bit of form."

Merse – "I can't believe that Gaz. I have had Leeds minus six. You honestly think Wigan by six?" (Merse is anxious and Marshall can see the fact that he has an opposite bet has upset him.)

Marshall – "Yes mate, that's why I backed it."

(Merson is being paid £1,800 for the evening)

Merse – "I am in for my whole fee. If I lose this bet I am on tonight for fuck all."

Marshall thinks I daren't tell him I have only bet a tenner.

Incredibly, Merson has bet his whole fee on a Rugby League game, to which Marshall nods and tells me he has been in the car with him when he is watching American Ladies Collegiate basketball that he has bet on.

Back to Penrith, and at half time Leeds are winning by six points, so both Merse and Marshall stand to lose.

Merse – "Right Gaz I have a signed Arsenal shirt in the boot. If you support Leeds and want them to win this game, you can have the shirt." (Such is the superstitious nature of an addict, clutching at straws.)

Marshall thinks – I am standing to win a tenner but if I don't and Merse wins I get a signed shirt. Nice!

So they stayed in the car with Marshall shouting at the radio with Merse. He feels with an extra person cheering and willing Leeds on, it will bring the bet the luck it needs.

"With two minutes to go it is going his way, I am winning a shirt and losing a tenner, and Merse is winning his £1,800, plus winnings. Then Wigan scored a try in the last minute so he lost it all. I won a tenner but I didn't see the shirt."

"So I am sitting next to him at the top table at this dinner knowing that he has driven all the way to Penrith, effectively for fuck all, because he has already gambled and lost his fee. I thought it was going to be dreadful, but like the professional he is, Merse just got up and did his speech and it was brilliant, as if nothing had happened."

Whenever they worked together Merson was always on his phone placing and following bets, but Marshall just feels he is the unluckiest gambler ever. Last year, a few weeks before Cheltenham, Merse told Marshall that he had been chatting with A P McCoy;

"Gaz, I was with Tony McCoy the other day and he told me that Annie Power could fall and still win."

As soon as the inevitable happened and one of the biggest favourites at the Festival did indeed fall, Marshall was quickly on the phone to console, (take the piss out of) his mate. Merse answered; 'Don't Gaz, please!' and hung up.

The other popular raconteur of all things Arsenal, with whom Marshall has the good fortune to tag-team with, is the Romford Pele, Ray Parlour. Parlour, for Marshall, could be a comedian himself, and is a natural story teller with an engaging delivery. Parlour is equally com-

Gary with ex-Gooner Ray Parlour

plimentary when it comes to Marshall: "I always look forward to working with Gaz, great company and a great act... and I'm not just saying that cos he's a Gooner!"

Many of Parlour's stories are well known, but Marshall shared a few of his personal favourites as a Gooner and a comedian.

Parlour's inadvertent involvement in the signing of Igor Stepanovs by Wenger it seems, was a practical joke that backfired. The Latvian had turned up at Colney for a trial and Parlour was standing watching him with a few of his colleagues, Martin Keown. He loudly observed what a class player he thought the trialist looked. Bergkamp, another of the squad's great jokers, quickly twigged what Parlour was up to and joined in and declared he could tell Igor was one of the best man-markers he had played against. Keown was bemused; 'what are you watching guys, he's rubbish!' Bergkamp responded by saying to Parlour that there was a 'touch of Beckenbauer about him.' At this point Keown was getting high pitched – 'No guys, honestly, he is really not that good.'

The assumption from Parlour is that Wenger, who was stood nearby, must have overhead the conversation, because the next minute he turned up as a signing. Marshall does his impression of Parlour doing his impression of Stepanovs – who sounds a lot like Borat – "It's good here, I like they give me plenty money." As Parlour concludes, "Arsene had been listening to us on the touchline not realising they were winding Keown up and he's only bloody signed him. £200,000 from Latvia, the worst player I have ever played with!"

A final classic from Marshall's time spent with Parlour concerns Arsenal's dark horse ecological entrepreneur businessman Mathieu Flamini. It appears the French midfield enforcer is set to be a billionaire from a green fuel that can replace conventional fossil fuels. However, according to the Romford Pele, in 2008, perhaps our Mathieu's financial brain was not so finely tuned when it came to money making.

Parlour had retired at the end of 2007, but was back at Arsenal training and keeping fit during the 2007/8 campaign with Wenger's blessing. One spring day he had been approached by Flamini, who had a favour to ask, he wanted Ray to help him set up a betting account. A simple request and easily done so; by the end of the day, Mathieu left Colney with a William Hill account and grateful to Parlour.

So, it was a surprised Parlour the following morning when he was confronted by an irate Flamini. The exchange went something like this:

Flamini – "Ray that stupid William Hill account does not work. They will not take my first bet."

Parlour – "What are you talking about mate? What was the bet they refused?"

Flamini – "£10,000 that my next club will be AC Milan and they say I cannot place zis bet."

Parlour – (laughing incredulously) "Of course you can't place a bet on yourself you idiot! What were you thinking of?"

Flamini – "I did not know zis. My brother needs some money so I was trying to help him."

Parlour (unsympathetically) – "Well if you are off to bloody Milan on a free given him some of your signing on fee!"

How about we sign off with Marshall's favourite gag? "I went to see a psychiatrist the other day. I said 'I have got an obsession with the film The Wizard of Oz.' He said 'why?' I said 'because, because, because, because...'"

ROMESH AND THE PUB LANDLORD

've heard it said that 'Romesh Ranganathan, he's on everything,' or 'He's never off our TV screens' but you can guarantee the person making the observation is doing so with a smile on their face. Of course, the phenomenal overnight success for Ranganathan has been anything but, and only a year before being nominated as the 'Best Newcomer' at the 2013 Edinburgh Festival the wannabe observational stand-up was still a full-time Maths teacher in West Sussex. His miserable hangdog expression and astutely comedic look at life were being honed in between parents evenings and bookmarking.

Getting to see his beloved Arsenal is not as regular as he would like now, due to his demanding work schedule, and I caught up with him a few months into a sell-out tour that will last around 10 months. Add to that his television commitments for the likes of *Mock the Week*, *Play to the Whistle*, his new show *It's not Rocket Science* and being a father to three young children. His reality may have changed with his success, but it was only four years ago that getting to the Emirates was tough for very different reasons.

"I think having kids makes it harder. For a while, just when we had our first two kids, before the comedy really started to take off, I was still teaching. When you are struggling and Arsenal tickets are as expensive as they are you can't justify it so much. I love it obviously."

In 2015 Ranganathan made the acclaimed documentary for the BBC 'Asian Provocateur' in which he, along with his mother, explored his Sri Lankan roots and ancestry. With both parents from cricket-mad Sri Lanka, one might assume, as I did, that perhaps the origin of his Arsenal support did not come from home. It would be safe to say that I assumed wrong.

RANGA AND SON

When his father arrived in England back in 1975, he lived in a cheap flat in Finchley and worked at KFC whilst finishing his account-ancy qualifications. Back then he was not really into sport, other than cricket; living where he was and wanting to 'fit in', his dad selected Arsenal. However, whilst he grew up in a household where football was increasingly important, they did not go to matches.

"To be honest with you dad looked at it and thought 'this isn't for us'. I think he felt it was at that time culturally not suitable. He watched it on TV and followed it in the papers but he didn't go to games. Bizarrely, years later, I took him to his first Arsenal game as I had started going before him."

Ironically his dad was *"much westernised and he became increas-ingly so, a proper big drinker. He got in amongst it I and did not keep himself to himself. He was always out with his work mates and would talk football, so it was odd that he never chose to actually go – but he was certainly very into the Gunners."*

I am not sure what it says about Ranganathan, or his dad, that the definition of being a proper westerner is being a proper drinker, but watching Arsenal in pubs certainly defined his father's Arsenal sup-port. The culture of watching football in pubs was to take on a further significance for the Ranganathan family later on. Certainly there was no choice for a young Romesh and his brother when it came to the family's football loyalties, even though by the time he arrived in 1978 his parents had moved to Crawley. *"Even my mum, who does not really know anything about football, is a Gooner."*

Everybody knew his dad simply as 'Ranga' and, after qualifying as an accountant, he went on to become the Finance Director for a book export company. Ultimately, he bought out the company, and bored of the commute, he moved the firm from Finchley to Crawley. Ranga began drinking at lunchtime in a pub down the road in East Grinstead. Why am I telling you this? Well, because Gooner Ranga got bored of book export, sold the company, bought the pub, became a pub land-lord and stayed one for the rest of his days.

You may guess what happened next. Not only was Ranga probably one of the only Sri Lankan pub landlords in the country, he swiftly con-verted 'The Prince of Wales,' sadly knocked down now, into an Arsenal pub. Ranganathan has many fond memories of watching Arsenal in the pub with his mates.

"It was so funny to watch Arsenal games in the pub. I used to go in with my mates, who thought my dad was a legend. He just would not tolerate any anti Arsenal chat. He adored Arsene Wenger and would not hear a word said against him in his pub. He was obsessive though, and I remember in 2005 Manchester United beat us 4-2 at Highbury on the back of ending our 49 match unbeaten run earlier in the season. The pub was absolutely rammed and at the end of the game my dad just walked up, turned off the TV and said 'Everybody fuck off!'" (I wish I could write those last three words in the voice of Ranganathan imper-sonating his dad in an exaggerated fashion.)

Romesh started going to Arsenal in his late teens, which we will come back to. His first game was in 1996 when he was 18, but he took Ranga to his first match in 2001. It was an FA Cup Fifth round tie against Chelsea at Highbury. He recalls being concerned how his temperamen-tal father might react in the tasty atmosphere of a London derby.

"I remember he was getting increasingly frustrated with Dennis Wise. What he did not realise I think, because you don't see it on the television, is just how annoying Dennis Wise was. In everyone's ear, niggling fouls and all that sort of shit and my Dad just could not cope with it and was getting so angry. He kept standing up and shouting 'Fuck off Wisey!' It was amazing just watching him, standing up and pointing and properly getting into it after all those years of supporting and not going."

Baby Romesh with his mum and dad

They had missed the kick off by a few minutes because Ranga had been really hungry, so they had stopped on the way to the ground. Ranga was not a healthy eater and the meal of choice on route to Highbury had been fried chicken. The Gunners had won, so began his father's tradition of having to eat fried chicken before every game thereafter.

A MAN WHO 'LOSES HIS SHIT' REGULARLY

Romesh's own first game was a 0-0 versus Liverpool in May 1996 – the game was pretty dull, but quite frankly, for Ranganathan, it barely mattered. Having seen them so much on television and been so into them, being there in the flesh just meant so much.

"I feel almost embarrassed to say that I had not been until I was 18, but that was just my upbringing. I envy friends of mine that had it, that you go to games and that's part of your childhood because I just don't have that. So when I did start going to be honest with you, the fact that I did not start going until later means that I am still a little bit of a kid when I go now. I am just buzzing every time I go and get properly excited."

He used to go to games with a friend of his dad's who could get tickets for him and a mate. One such occasion was for the visit of Aston Villa before Christmas in December 2001. It was the season that Arsenal secured their second League and FA Cup Double under Wenger, but on this occasion, they did not make it easy for themselves. The Gunners went 2-0 down and had not managed to reply by half-time. To make matters worse the opening Villa strike had come from Paul Merson. Ranganathan recalls the epic fight-back with goals from Wiltord and Henry, before Thierry smashed in his second to win it for the Arsenal. It is those dramatic moments that make football like no other sport.

"I just lost my shit, like properly lost my shit, to the point where I can't remember ever feeling an emotion anything like that. You know I am a staid, chilled out, grumpy, indifferent sort of guy in everyday life. So I don't really get like that anywhere else. I love my music and I even when I go and see really amazing music I never get like that. It is the climatic nature of the game that gets you like that. Games like that are just the perfect storm for really losing your shit and it does not happen to you anywhere else. There is just no excitement like the moments your team can give you."

For Ranganathan the night Henry returned for Arsenal is another perfect example of how only football can provide such a euphoric moment. The game itself was a dull affair, but the Henry goal, and the immediate aftermath, will live with every Arsenal fan forever. As he says, only football really does that.

BLOODY MICHAEL OWEN AND BLOODY SOUTHERN SCOUSERS

Of course the nature of football works both ways and the climax can often be enjoyed by someone else, so to speak! In Cardiff, in May 2001, it was Liverpool fans 'losing their shit' and that was not a good day for Ranganathan, in so many ways.

A friend from Kingston University had managed to secure two tickets for the Cup Final. His mate was a Liverpool fan but the tickets were in the Arsenal end, so Ranganathan was hugely excited. The day did not start well with him and his pal rather naively arriving at Paddington without booking train tickets in advance. An obvious school boy, or in this case, 'student' error. They asked a staff member when the next train to Cardiff was, and when the reply was 'which one have you get tickets for?', the realisation of their stupidity began to sink in. Particularly when the reply to their next question, 'can't we just buy tickets on the train?' got the withering look it deserved. They were told there was a queue they could join. Feeling slightly better that there were other complete idiots they went to find the queue in the direction the guys had pointed. That feeling did not last more than a few seconds when they saw the lines of other idiots was almost the length of the station.

"We were in a queue, but it is moving so slowly and I said to my mate 'I can't believe this, we have got tickets for the fucking FA Cup Final and we are not going to get there because we are twats!'

With despair growing, Ranganathan heard a man behind them in the slow moving queue on his phone: *'Do you know darling I don't think I am going to get on this train. Do you know what I am going to do sweetheart I am going to grab my car and drive.'*

Desperate times call for desperate measures and he just turned around to this chap, who he did not know from Adam, and said *"If we pay all your petrol money will you take us with you to Cardiff?"*

Luckily for the hapless pair the kindly chap agreed; unluckily as it transpired for Ranganathan, he was another southern Scouser. The banter was relaxed and amusing on the way to Wales, and on offering further food and petrol money, the friendly guy agreed to bring them back as well.

Well we all know what happened next, Michael Owen committed daylight robbery to steal a game Arsenal had dominated. The nature of the defeat was so gutting for Gooners, but providing the Liverpool supporters with their own climatic moment. Ranganathan's mate asked if he wanted to leave but he magnanimously allowed his friend to stay for the FA Cup presentation, standing silently in the emptying Arsenal end. The friendly generosity soon ended as the two met up with their lift back to London.

"I had to listen to those two arseholes the whole way back to London. There is nothing worse than a gloating Liverpool fan who is not even a Scouser. Oh yes there are 2 gloating Liverpool fans who aren't even Scousers! They dropped me in London and I got the train back to Crawley, called a mate and said 'can we just go out and get pissed I am so depressed about this result and have had the journey from hell!'"

ARSENAL AND EXPECTATIONS IN OBSERVATIONAL STAND UP

Many of those I have interviewed talked about how tricky it is to mention football as part of their acts. Once you are well known as a Gooner, the subject matter can be dangerous and invites controversy and antagonism. Earlier in his career, before audiences knew of his footballing allegiance, Edinburgh 2013, Ranganathan's observations about his personal relationship with his fandom and Arsenal formed part of his routine – some personal thoughts and other fans' relationships with his team might seem alien to some, but very familiar to others.

The thought process that ended up in his act began when the Gunners period of dominance, and constantly competing in the early Wenger years, came to an end. He recalls being in the car driving one day, probably in 2006, and for the first time in years the top teams in the run in for the title were being mentioned, and Arsenal were not being talked about. After the initial shock, he began to feel that, actually, there was a strange possibility that football may be more interesting to him.

"During the unbeaten season, we either having expected to win, or we drew and were mildly disappointed. I guess we all just took things for granted."

If your expectations through a period of inconsistency, or below par performances, are lowered, the highs might just get higher. The overall contentment might essentially be lowered as a whole, but the unanticipated, or surprise, successes give rise to more euphoria.

"I remember a game at Stamford Bridge where we went 1-0 down to Chelsea. We equalised and then Robin van Persie scored and we won 2-1, (even though the guy is now a twat) I remember the huge feeling of elation, which was heightened because of the expectation that we were going to get beat. Sometimes I wonder (and I talked about this on stage) if sometimes you want your team to be a little bit up and down. It gives you more of a story and can be a bit more exciting. I just think that football gives you a drama that you simply don't get in any other aspect of life."

He also talked in the Edinburgh show about the irrational impact Arsenal can have on you as an individual, and how it is totally out of line with any real perspective. When I asked Romesh to elaborate he cites the example of today – a day on which Arsenal have just drawn 0-0 away to Sunderland who are in the bottom three.

"Basically, I will be on my way to a tour show (like today) and I have got the match on the radio, but if we have a bad result, I am so gutted

and I wonder if I am going to be alright for the show. Something that has happened so far away, involving people who don't know me or give a shit about me, whose lives have no cross-over with mine, gets to me so much, it's mental. Although trust me Alex Brooker is far worse than me."

In the Edinburgh show he explored how, perhaps, he had become complacent as an Arsenal fan, during the peak of the Wenger success, because the team was always winning. He thought at the time he was happy, but actually, wondered whether he was massively indifferent. He recalls fans moaning about having to travel to Cardiff 'again' and being appalled, but considers that the mentality behind it is born out of ridiculously raised expectation levels.

"I think it is true of anything in life and where your expectations are low or lowered and something good happens you appreciate it so much more."

IS THE LAST BASTION OF TRIBALISM BEING DILUTED?

One of the most depressing things Ranganathan observed, as a teacher in 21st century England, was an increasingly worrying trend of football allegiances changing. He noticed it particularly when Chelsea came to the fore in Mourinho's first spell in charge – blue shirts spread like wildfire in Crawley and in his school. Suddenly, kids who had been Brighton or Crawley, were Chelsea fans

"I know I am guilty of it too, because I am Crawley born and bred, but my dad was from North London and it was passed on, as it should be. I recall thinking it was such a shame because football is the last bastion of tribalism in a way. You don't have Mods, Punks and Rockers, so what you have is football, and that is being eroded because kids go with the flow."

He recalls a Parent's Evening at school when the dad sitting in front of him was a West Ham fan – the previous term both had been Hammers, but the son had switched to Chelsea.

"I was like 'Dude, West Ham is exactly the type of club that need to be holding on to their fans and grooming the next generation. Why are you letting your son change to Chelsea?'"

He even recalls one of the worst examples was when he was covering a class, and because he was unfamiliar with the boys, he asked them what teams they supported. One lad had said 'Real Madrid' so he asked him, 'Yeah, but which English team?' The kid just had looked at the teacher oddly and replied 'No, just Real Madrid.'

As a teacher, Romesh was very open and proud of his Arsenal support, so the stick he had to take on Monday mornings if the Gunners lost would be unbearable. Nevertheless, in his own home, the family are left in no doubt about the Ranganathan loyalties. The third generation certainly know the score!

"Obviously I have said to my children, well, not the youngest who is only one, but to the other two, you are Arsenal. As far as I am concerned they are Arsenal fans and we are an Arsenal family. My wife is not a huge football fan, but she gets it, and allows my silliness – the Arsenal Babygros and bibs saying 'I dribble for the Gunners' and all that shit."

FALLING IN LOVE WITH IAN WRIGHT AND MEETING YOUR HEROES

"My earliest strong emotions in an Arsenal sense was falling in love with Ian Wright. I thought he was so exciting, I loved everything about him. I loved the way he carried himself on the pitch. I loved his goals and his celebrations. I loved all the shit between him and Peter Schmeichel. I loved the fact he pulled up his shirt on the wrong goal when he got the record. I loved everything about him, I thought he was a Rock Star. I just totally fell in love with him."

At the end of 2015 he was on tour supporting his friend, Scottish comedian, Kevin Bridges, and staying at a Manchester hotel. It was the morning after the day and night before, which had consisted of the Manchester derby and then 'going out and getting absolutely battered'. He was sitting in the hotel lobby, feeling like death, with Bridges only mildly better, and it would be safe to say not feeling overly conversational.

Perhaps it was not the ideal time to spot Ian Wright, sitting with some other people just across the lobby. Bridges, knowing how his mate felt about 'Wrighty', asked if he was going to go over and introduce himself to his hero?

"I said 'I'm just hungover Kev, I just don't want to be like this when I meet Ian Wright. I just have to believe there will be another occasion. I am too nervous and I can't even talk properly.' I guess I was thinking what's worse than not meeting him now, is meeting him and making a complete knob of myself, and knowing forever that Ian Wright thinks I am a twat."

Rom, Rambo and some other bloke?

Unfortunately, or fortunately perhaps, as they made to leave, Wright looked over and made eye contact so the pair had to go and chat. As it transpired Wright had seen Ranganathan's show *Asian Provocateur* and said something along the lines of 'You're the guy who did that show where you went to Sri Lanka.'

"I nearly stared crying, thinking Ian Wright knows who I am. Then I was just like a gibbering wreck. It's crazy because doing stand-up I have gigged with people that have been my heroes, like Jack Dee and Bill Burr, and even around those guys I am myself, but there is something different about when I meet footballers. With Wrighty I was nervous and talked shit. I remember chatting to Ian Stone afterwards and asked him to apologise to Wrighty if I had come across as an idiot."

Romesh also got to meet Aaron Ramsey, Alex Oxlade-Chamberlain and Calum Chambers when they did something for the *Rocket Science* show he does for ITV. For Ranganathan, though, he classes that as very different to meeting Ian Wright, because they weren't playing for Arsenal in his formative years as a Gooner.

"It's like the music you listen to in a certain period of your life will always have more resonance. The present Arsenal team simply does not resonate with me as much as previous teams."

Although readers will be pleased to hear there was still a Ranganathan *'lose my shit'* moment with Ramsey. There was a stunt where they had to pull a double decker bus along with the FA Cup. He was holding the Cup with Ramsey, then turned to the Welshman and said; *'I can't believe I am holding the FA Cup with you.'*

"I momentarily let my cynical mask slip and became an excited Arsenal fan, holding the Cup with one of the players... a nice moment."

He explains that even when Arsenal players come on shows he finds himself naturally willing them on to do well and encouraging them. Oxlade-Chamberlain came on *Play to the Whistle* and he found he was nervous for the young Gunner. He finds himself in his natural environment, where comedy is crucial to the success of the show, more the father figure, or a teacher looking out for his boys.

"I want an Arsenal lad to look good. I was the same with Ramsey when he came on League of their Own, encouraging him and complimenting him, saying that was wicked. It's just because I have a greater connection with them than perhaps other guests. It is like having a mate on the show. I hope they come across well, and if there is an opportunity for me to tee them up with something, I will take it."

On a comedy panel show, Ranganathan is king, but he was not quite so impressive and controlled when meeting one Arsenal hero. He recalls totally embarrassing himself when working at Sunglasses Hut in the South Terminal of Gatwick Airport – a part-time job while paying his way through University. Given the location, you would often see famous people, and one day spotted Arsenal's new star signings, David Platt, meandering around the shops. Plucking up courage and a plan, he asked a colleague to hold the fort while he ran to the book shop across the way to buy the first Arsenal book he could lay his hands on, while Platt was browsing.

"Then, when Platt ventured into Sunglasses Hut, I said 'Can I get your autograph please?' Then, as he was signing it, I said, for no reason other than I was a total knob, "I am the biggest Arsenal fan in the whole world!" He just looked at me in a withering way and said 'Okay mate' and left the shop as quickly as he could!"

THE ARSENAL COMEDIANS NETWORK

So, an obvious question to ask is when there are so many Gooners in his world, and particularly on *Mock the Week,* do they all go to the pub and argue about Arsene Wenger like the rest of us? There must have been occasions when Ranganathan, Dara O'Briain, Hugh Dennis and Rob Beckett have all been on the show together.

He is good friends with Rob Beckett, and they sometime go to matches together – but yes, Romesh, Dara and Rob do frequently get told off for holding up filming whilst they dissect the previous match.

"There was one time Dara got massively excited because he had tweeted Podolski who had replied by sending him a message. He had

not even realised the German was following him and he was showing us the message – Rom, Rom look at that!!"

Ultimately, because of the nature of the job and the demands, fellow comedians do become close friends. Essentially, they are his work colleagues, they are no different to the rest of us and as fans they love nothing better than chatting about their team. He ventures that it is why so many were happy to talk about their relationship with Arsenal for this book. Because Romesh does not have a season tickets or membership that some of the others have, if he finds himself free at short notice for a home match, it is to the 'comedians network' that he often turns to for assistance.

As with any group of fellow Gooners, not all views are the same and the debates can be intense and interesting. As for Ranganathan, he does understand fans of other clubs who think Arsenal fans are a tad spoilt and expectant, but equally, he empathises and shares the frustrations.

"There are so many different variables, and while I am a big fan of Wenger, I do think that Arsenal basically suggesting he is unsackable is a big mistake. Even if you think that, you have to have somebody feel they are accountable for what happens. Otherwise people can get a 'God complex' and I believe we have seen that emerge with Wenger."

NEVER BEEN AS PROUD AS IN 1998

Ranganathan still ranks the run-in of 1997/98 as his favourite time as a Gooner. Arsenal were 13 points behind Manchester United and went on that amazing run to over-take Ferguson's fabulous team – Wenger had arrived and made his mark in his first full season – blending a strong existing Arsenal core, primarily a great defence, with stunning new signings.

"I think it was the most amazing thing. Winning that title was just the best feeling as a fan and I can't imagine ever getting tired of that feeling, even if we did it every year. It was the drama of it, the Overmars goal at Old Trafford, going through the emotions and the fact that we had been so far behind. It was just incredible and I remember buzzing for ages afterwards. I covered my car in Arsenal shit. I wanted everyone to know I was a Gooner, I was so proud."

"I was so upset when we sold Petit and Overmars to Barcelona – the break-up of the greatest team I have ever seen. That '98 side will be with me until the day I die."

Despite what Arsenal went on to achieve in 2002 and 2004, many fans will appreciate and share that view, and given what Ranganathan has told us about his support, it should not surprise us. Because the culmination of the 1997/98 season combined the 'climatic nature' of football he so eloquently described, with the heightened elation derived when expectations are low and massively exceeded, as he discussed on stage in Edinburgh in 2013. Being 13 points and five places off top spot at Christmas, to go on a run to end with the 4-0 home win, with that Tony Adams goal, and then to win the FA Cup, certainly ticks all his boxes.

THE REASONS I REALLY HATE ARSENAL

I n a book all about funny guys' love and passion for all things Arsenal, somehow, Alan Davies convinced me it would be funnier still if I asked a Spurs supporting comic to write a balancing anti-Gunner rant.

Of course, due to the relative popularity and success of the near neighbours in North London (Arsenal) and Middlesex (Tottenham) finding one in the first place is tricky. However, after an extensive search I am 'sort of' delighted to say that award winning stand-up, Edinburgh veteran and Podcast partner to Chris Martin, Carl Donnelly stepped up. When I say I am only 'sort of' delighted, the 'sort of' part came after I had read what Carl had to say. Because as anti-Arsenal rants go, the following is annoyingly well constructed. Oh well, they have to be good at something I guess.

In Henry V, Shakespeare wrote; "There is no more faith in thee than in a stewed prune –" I think this is a good starting point to discuss my feelings towards Arsenal. A football club is, as anyone who understands football knows, a complex organism made up by those in charge; the players, the ground and the staff, but in the centre of all that, its beating heart are its fans. No club can function without a passionate, loyal fanbase that respects itself as well as the club's history. To nurture such a fanbase, you need loyalty and respect in the other direction from the club.

This is where Arsenal have, as a club and a fanbase, repeatedly destroyed any chance of being a 'proper' club over the course of their history. Their constant moving of grounds (ok, it's twice in 100 years but still) in the hope of a better life, with little care for the fans, but all thoughts on money, disrespects the very nature of the sport as being that of the people. They are the U2 of football clubs, claiming to care and love the people, while counting their cash and laughing behind closed doors. I can imagine Stan Kroenke diving into his pool of money like Scrooge McDuck, while naive Arsenal fans outside pay for the most expensive season tickets in the world while talking about how great it is that the club has "financial stability".

The club's relationship with its fans over the last ten years has bordered on abusive. Each year the fans are told the club will change and spend some of its millions on players, to bring glory to the new ground (which has the atmosphere of Christmas dinner after your granddad says something racist) and, like battered wives, the Arsenal fans lap it up and tell their friends "He's changed, really!" while we all look on from the outside with pity knowing that, like all abusive relationships, the abused need to fully realise their torture in order to escape.

With their legion of ex-players now whoring themselves around the networks as below average pundits singing the praises of the club and its hierarchy, the fans will never see that their club is first and foremost a business and a football club second.

Now, obviously I am biased (before you tweet me saying "Well you would say that, you're a scummy Spurs fan"). As a fan of the only genuinely great North London club, it is to be assumed that I have an irrational hatred of the Gooners, but let me just clarify that my dislike for them goes way beyond irrationality. It is the result of 34 years of experience and in-depth research and analysis and is very, very rational. It's also an organic, ever-changing hatred that dates back to the boring Arsenal days, has gone through the thuggery of 'The Invincibles' and now looks on with a sense of pity at Wenger's selection of soft bellied wusses who ponce around the field with the physical integrity of dandelions.

The one constant throughout every era of Arsenal has been the overwhelming sense of entitlement and delusion running through the veins of the 'fans'. During the 2016 season, following the yearly Christmas collapse, in which they threw away what should have been their first title since 2003-4, Paul Merson, while bemoaning their lack of form, claimed "Arsenal are the best team in the world when the pressure is off". Now there is a lot wrong with this claim, so let's go through it in parts.

First, it is being made by Paul Merson, a man whose ability to talk shite is unparalleled. In one of his finest pieces of punditry he once said; "There's only one person gets you sacked and that's the fans". Don't get me wrong, he was an excellent player (and I say that through gritted teeth) but the jump to punditry tends not to be related to on-field ability (see Michael Owen for a prime example of this) so his claims of Arsenal's world beating ability are not to be taken too seriously.

Secondly, it's just plain wrong. In a world where Barcelona are currently fielding a front line of Messi, Suarez and Neymar, to say that an Arsenal team with Olivier Giroud are the "best team in the world" is an incredible claim. When a third of your starting eleven wouldn't make the West Ham team I think it's time to wind your necks in and quieten down.

Finally on this subject, it is based on an absolute falsehood that there is ever a time in football that is without pressure. In the last decade, there have been non-stop claims from ex-Arsenal players and fans alike that Arsenal play great football, but ultimately fail to get the results, and it is down to some inability to deal with pressure. The truth of the matter is that Arsenal are simply not as good as they think, and a top four finish each year and the potential of a domestic cup, is pretty much the most they deserve based on the quality of their team. There is no added pressure on Arsenal that isn't also piled on to every other team fighting for a league, Champions League place, cup or survival, so to blame this for the players' lack of ability is a way of diverting attention away from the truth that you're just a bit shit.

The entitlement and arrogance doesn't only appear in the stands but it's also a recurring theme with your players. We all know that Chelsea are the go-to club for most of football's biggest wankers, but I think it's safe to say that Arsenal will happily hoover up the dregs of the arseholes left in the transfer market.

Spurs, as you may know, pride themselves on a selection of well behaved, polite, humble, nice young men. This is partially down to our strong Belgian contingent who, as we know, are the most well-mannered of all the nations. Arsenal should take note and draft in a few Belgians to have a word with your current enfant terrible Jack Wilshere, who carries himself in his day-to-day life with all the grace of a pissed up best man on a stag do. On the pitch he no doubt has some ability (even if his plan of attack in each match is to try and set the world record for the most unnecessary Cruyff turns in 90 minutes) but it's his petulance and off field behaviour that causes the most shame on his club.

With an injury record similar to Samuel L Jackson's character in 'Unbreakable', Jack obviously spends a lot of time in recovery and, where most players see this as a time of gentle reflection and rehabilitation, he clearly sees it differently. Rather than spend his days with the physio and nights with his feet up watching box sets, Jack would rather spread the word on his revolutionary new recovery method of getting shit faced, having a dust up in a night club and chain smoking Marlborough Lights. And it seems to be working because with this new system it only takes him nine months to recover from cramp, playing two full matches, then pulling up 15 minutes into training with gout!

It's not Jack's fault, of course, he is just maintaining the tradition of each Arsenal squad having at least one 'wrong un' at any time. The list of Arsenal cheats over the years is pretty impressive when you scan through. To name just a few from the Premier League era you of course had Thierry Henry whose shameless handball for France was the worst thing to happen to Ireland since the Black and Tans (Donnelly is an Irish name in case you were wondering why I'm bitter about this), Cesc Fabregas with his Tom Daley-esque diving ability, Patrick Viera who left no cheekbone unelbowed and Martin Keown who isn't kidding anyone with his Mr Nice guy act on the BBC nowadays.

To conclude, I just want to say that everything above is obviously written through the prism of bias and is mostly tongue in cheek*. I'm as aware of that as you. I am a proud Spurs fan who has been raised to have an ingrained dislike for everything Arsenal (to be honest, it's only out of politeness that I'm using the name Arsenal and not Woolwich, which is obviously your real name) but I mean this from the heart when I say that I truly enjoy the rivalry our two teams have.

We are defined by our enemies and some of my greatest footballing memories (good and bad) are of North London derbies. We will keep being Spurs, a classy, exciting, respected team full of good people, run for its fans by people that really care, and you keep being Arsenal, a multi-national corporation managed by an old French weirdo with a disdain for its own fans (who are mostly knob-heads). Keep up the good work Gooners.

Carl Donnelly
*It's not. I meant every word of it.

I would like to thank Carl for this amusing interlude and for what can only be described as a personal therapy session. I hope you enjoy the short move within Middlesex while your own club moves stadium!

TOM ROSENTHAL, FRIDAY NIGHT OBSESSIVE GOONER

The last five years have been pretty amazing for Tom Rosenthal. Within a year of graduating in Philosophy from Kings College London he had been nominated for 'Breakthrough Comedian of the Year,' jointly won the Leicester Mercury Comedian of the Year prize and secured a role in Channel 4's fabulous instantly cult sitcom hit 'Friday Night Dinner.' In 2016 he is still on our screens weekly, starring in the third series of BAFTA nominated 'Plebs,' accurately described as a cross between Up Pompeii and Blackadder. Tom is also the son of legendary TV sports presenter Jim. His father, as we shall discover, has been a significant influence in Tom's life but crucially we can be grateful to him for his latitude and understanding when Arsenal's greater calling beckoned a young Tom.

TOM, JIM AND DENNIS

So the obvious question is how does the son of a high profile and diehard Oxford fan Jim Rosenthal end up a home and away Gooner? Well the reason for not adopting Oxford despite his dad, actually came from said dad. Jim was of the view that where possible a young football fan growing up should support their local team. In Tom's case, born in

West London, his dad decided that this team should be Queens Park Rangers. He recollects being taken to QPR on three or four occasions aged five or so. His father even had him fully kitted out in the famous hoops and taken to the training ground. He even still has a photo from this trip where he is being held by Rangers legend Les Ferdinand. It seemed however, that his father's attempts to get his son to engender some kind of relationship with his local team were doomed to failure.

Young Tom found himself naturally more invested in Oxford and there are times he feels his dad perhaps should have laid down the law to support the family team. He certainly enjoyed his trips to the old Manor Ground more than his excursions to Loftus Road. It felt more natural being with his father and other family and friends whereas being at QPR seemed slightly mechanistic.

"So despite the fact that QPR were supposed to be my team it just never gelled with me. I did not feel the attachment or the excitement. It did not feel right or fundamental to my relationship with football that I supported QPR and I felt more connected to Oxford."

At the same time as the visits to his supposed team and the more enjoyable trips to the Manor Ground, because of his dad's job he was able to go to so many other stadia. Most weekends either with work or through friends and connections Tom was accompanying his dad to one match or another. He recalls going to Palace, Fulham, Wimbledon and further afield to Newcastle and Southampton. Then aged six, because of Jim Rosenthal's closer working relationship with Arsenal legend Bob Wilson who had moved to ITV in 1994, he was taken to Highbury.

"I remember sitting at Highbury and thinking this place is a bit different to all other football grounds I had experienced. It did feel a cut above, incredibly historic and you just felt special being there."

Coupled with the fact that the Rosenthals had spent their first few years as a young family living in Canonbury, Highbury instinctively felt much more like home. Fate was playing its hand and a seven year old Tom began asking his dad if it might be acceptable to change one's football team. Jim of course was a serious football man and offered his son a considered football man's answer.

"He told me I could change the team I supported once but only once, so I had to be certain because if you change again you are NOT a football fan. He basically gave me a get out of jail card. I think he realised that your club has to come from your heart and out of your sense of

Rosenthal performs at the Comedy store

Tom's tenth birthday at Highbury with Jim and friends

community which he had with Oxford but I had moved around and had not found with QPR."

Despite his tender age Tom was already an obsessive sports watcher. He was for example obsessed with Alan Donald, the South African fast bowler and his bowling action. He would practice Donald's technique, attempting to replicate it in his back garden. Similarly as a six year old he had watched the whole of the 1994 World Cup in America and with no England to follow, he had found himself drawn to a certain Dutch genius. As with Donald he was drawn to the perfect technique. He describes Dennis as his favourite player ever. *"If there was a football textbook he was it."*

"So I felt this tie, I had been to the ground, sensed it was a bit different and special and then we signed Dennis Bergkamp. I was pretty much like 'yup, that's my team. So basically my dad let me get away

with it and I became an Arsenal fan. I don't regret it funnily enough and I have never looked back longingly at QPR and thought if only..."

PERFORMING STAND-UP IN A CROWD
OR BEING IN THE ARSENAL CROWD?

Rosenthal's passion for public speaking and ultimately performing as a stand-up was born at his *'nice posh school'*. As he explained, if you go to a school where there are competitions for doing speeches and all these posh parents applaud you and tell you are wonderful little cherubs, you do begin to believe it. Even if the truth is that you are just marginally better than the next boy, who is incidentally terrible.

"So after I left I decided I still needed the attention that posh parents had given me, so I opted to seek it in pub basements. Slightly less receptive audiences of course, made up of drunken men calling me a prick, as opposed to posh parents giving me awards."

He agrees that to try and be a comedian *'you have to be a bit mental actually'* and have a strange drive to put yourself through what you have to. It is a hard school where the only way to improve and learn your trade is in front of crowds who may not like you or all your material. Again Rosenthal credits his school and his broadcaster father.

"Having a slightly sheltered upbringing where people were giving me the confidence to express myself almost certainly helped. Also, having my dad who was obviously very much in the public eye helped because you could see that even though he was very well respected, in general he would also get a lot of shit."

Twitter today illustrates the point perfectly where anyone who is well known for anything will get as many people calling them a prick as praising them, he contends. If you want to make it as a stand-up comedian you just have to deal with it.

"So I think maybe even if I was not totally prepared to have a lot of drunk people calling me a cunt I was sort of expecting it. Maybe having a dad in the public eye both drove me to and prepared me for doing stand-up comedy."

Whilst being busy doing television at present has prevented him doing a gig for about nine months, Rosenthal is certainly not about to abandon the skill he has honed over years at university and beyond. He would love to make television for his whole career but is under no illusion that may well not be a reality. So his ability to make people laugh with just a mic is something he will maintain as best he can. He admires those who can flit between television and stand-up citing his own inability to concentrate on multiple projects.

"I am very bad at concentrating on more than one thing at a time which is sort of why I love football as much as I do. Because whether I am playing it or watching it you can forget about literally everything else and be lost in your enjoyment of the game."

When comparing the two worlds he loves; is it possible to compare the exhilaration of a successful stand-up performance, where he is the star receiving the appreciation, to the exhilaration of being in a crowd at an Arsenal game where a crucial goal has been scored? Huge laughter and applause at a Tom Rosenthal gig compared to the Welbeck winner on his comeback versus Leicester perhaps?

"Some comedians say they never feel as alive as when they're on stage, but for me I just generally feel quite anxious! There is an anxiety obviously linked to a show going badly, but likewise when it goes well. I am not too good with too much praise. I am not like Ronaldo, standing there chest out saying I am the best. When I'm watching the football crowd it's nice that that anxiety is proliferated. So everyone feels the tension when Theo Walcott miscontrols it for the 30th time, but everyone felt the release when Welbeck scored that incredible goal. I virtually passed out."

So genuinely nearly fainted? According to Rosenthal one second after the ball hit the back of the net, he was bundling with everyone in celebration, the next he found himself shivering, short of breath and sitting on the ground. He describes it as the most intense moment he can remember at the Emirates and a near religious experience. This brings us back to the crowd-heightened sense of the experience.

"If a player scored a great goal on the training pitch they may get excited but not as excited as when they score a goal in front of 60,000 people, the vast majority of whom are also willing it to go in. It's why football for me, not being particularly religious, is the ultimate sort of sociological group experience. You are just fundamentally desperate for this meaningless thing to happen that because of the environment becomes enormously meaningful."

Sticking with the quasi-religious experiences that football can give us Rosenthal's favourite Emirates goal before the Welbeck one was when Thierry Henry came back. It did feel like a second coming, the return of the messiah and did feel spectacularly religious. It was so peculiar like watching your memories live before your eyes and not reliving them in your head.

"This may sound like a weird thing to bring up but you know with Prince having just died, people are saying I wish I had seen him live. So with Henry after he left you are thinking I wish I could see it one more time or perhaps if you had never actually seen him live and then he came back and he did it in exactly the same majestic way."

WE'VE GOT MESUT OZIL

This was certainly a quote that came up in research that required elaboration. *'My lock screen is a picture of Mesut Ozil and my home screen a picture of my girlfriend. I love them both equally.'*

Fortunately his partner is supportive of his love of Arsenal and is not at all offended by the fact that Mesut Ozil is the only player ever likely to compete with Dennis as Rosenthal's favourite Gunner. Whilst recognising he has done far less at this stage for Arsenal, he is the only one to come close to the Iceman's vision and poise.

Rosenthal's summation of Ozil's brilliance could not be more original. He likes to feel, because he is arrogant (his words), that he has watched enough football to think he can play a match or sequence of play out in his mind, like FIFA. He explains that as a kid he would do a very strange thing when sitting watching matches at Highbury.

"The people that used to go with me thought I had some sort of 'Rain Man' affectation where I used to sit and map out how I thought the play should develop with my hands."

He would be mapping out the play sequence in his head and acting it out with his hands – you pass to him, you pass on to him and then you move to there to receive etc. He quickly adds that he had to get out of that habit because people thought him, frankly, a weird little kid. He still does his weird little kid thing, but in his head. He watches play evolve, sees a pattern of play and thinks where the ball should go and how play should develop. He suggests that obviously playing football FIFA style in your mind should be pretty easy if you can sit up in the stands, see the whole picture and anticipate where the passes should go. Indeed sometimes you should be able to predict it better than the players on the pitch as you can see far more than they can.

"But Mesut will regularly make passes that you just cannot see, even in the stands. That is why he is ahead of so many defenders but

sadly he is also ahead of his own strikers most of the time. Giroud often has not got a clue and it is why I feel so sorry for him sometimes. It is like steak service with burger strikers!"

Rosenthal simply loves watching our German genius. He would go as far as to say that with some of the chips and swerves he puts on the ball he seems, like Bergkamp, to have reinventing passing in a way.

"Even just what look like simple touches to create space or that thing he does where he flicks the ball over tackles. I have never seen anyone else do that and he does it so easily. It is like Bergkamp says in his book he hates players doing tricks as affectations without any goal to it. I think Ozil is the same. He is just a joy to watch and you can guarantee that every game he will do something that is worth the ticket price."

PODCASTS AND THE 'SEARING ANGER OF INJUSTICE!'

Being aware that Rosenthal has guested on the 'Footballistically' podcast, what are his general views on the Arsenal fans' apparent obsession with the pod?

This question takes us off in a different direction as he has strong personal views on what they achieve which can be highly negative or certainly has been of late. He does not listen to Gunner pods often because they essentially just serve up what he can happily or unhappily overhear in the ground or listen to and participate in with mates in the pub post-match. Very much his father's son, he would rather read considered impartial journalism than listen to fans moaning as to why we should not have lost the match and whose fault it was.

Rosenthal says he recognises the passionately vitriolic fan from his own adolescence, and that in his twenties has tried to sit back and enjoy his football and his team by not getting too worked up when things don't go as planned.

"I used to be the traditional football fan, very angry, and I think I realised maybe five years ago, that level of anger does not serve your life or health particularly well."

This question was one he had been dwelling on in advance of the meeting and he has a fabulous example of the why he made the decision to stop allowing football to get to him as much as it once did. It goes back to an away trip to Dortmund in 2002 and a 14 year old Rosenthal who made the trip with his dad. Arsenal lost the game 2-1 and the game turned on a penalty decision given by controversial

Spanish referee, Mejuto Gonzalez. The Germans scored the penalty to win the game after Seaman was alleged to have brought down Jan Koller. An adolescent Rosenthal could not control how angry he was because there had been 'no contact' on the Czech striker who had conned Gonzalez. After the match he was to see the awful referee checking in at his own hotel.

"I was incensed and considering all the things I could do. I dunno, ring his hotel phone and breathe down it like a psycho or order fifty portions of mackerel on his room-service. I spent ten minutes trying to find a bag I could shit in to leave outside his room. I didn't do anything in the end of course but I still remember that searing anger of injustice."

Rosenthal went on to say that because he had been coming for this interview, he had, for the first time in 14 years watched the highlights of the match on YouTube. With much laughter he admits it was a definite penalty and that Seaman had blatantly taken Koller out. This is of course the lesson here because the level of injustice is always with the angry football fan. Yet it is ridiculous because 90% of the time in the stadium you are so far away you cannot possibly see if a decision is correct or otherwise. He therefore endeavours to keep his inner football fan in check although on occasion the 'anger of injustice' does re-emerge. Last season, when Costa got Gabriel sent off would be a case in point.

"A lot of football fans feel that level of injustice and the resulting anger every game and that is an emotion I prefer not to feel. I don't really want to be considering shitting in bags and leaving it outside people's rooms, no matter what they have done."

Like all great observational stand-up comedians, having taken an amusing diversion into a seemingly alternative subject, Rosenthal brings us back to the original point. The podcast phenomenon he suggests sometimes can perpetuate the anger and feelings of injustice and keep fans wound up. Arsenal Fan TV is a prime protagonist and for him they are just giving a voice to the annoying know it all fan; all of us have at least one sitting behind us, who always know better than the manager and the player and have to shout out inane advice continuously; why are you passing it there? Stop fannying around and get it in the box... blah blah blah!

"Some fans clearly feel entitled to pass comment but why? There's a man behind me who will constantly shout 'Pass! Shoot! Kick it!' You

don't go to a play and shout 'Act it! Act it! Cry!' - You are there to watch
them. They are the uniquely skilled ones. You're just a bloke with high
blood pressure and eight quid fish and chips. For me football is a pas-
sion and we have to enjoy these remarkable human beings as much as
we can. Otherwise what's the point?"

FOOTBALL KIT ASPERGER'S

You may be getting the impression by now of Tom Rosenthal, Arsenal fan, overly obsessed in some aspects of his support and chilled
and relaxed in others. With football kits we are back to the obsessed
Rosenthal.

An avid collector of football shirts since his dad used to bring them
home for him as a boy. To the point that he found himself having recurring dreams of Jim arriving with a new and special shirt. His dream was
also his reality as he pretty much got a kit from every match his dad
was reporting on.

"I definitely used to get every new Arsenal shirt and it was essential
that I had the correct style of number on the back. Because in the early
years of the Premier League it wasn't the standardised numbers and
you would sometimes get the wrong number style on the wrong shirt,
and that would greatly upset me. I was a sheltered child. The worst
thing that happened in my upbringing was a mismatched Nike theme,
it's hardly Oliver Twist."

Unfortunately the desire for accuracy on the shirt extended to the
'ROSENTHAL' name in the correct font and lettering on the reverse.
He soon discovered that adult Gooners did not always respect his per-
fect home shirt with the correct number and letter style when Ronnie
Rosenthal had the same number and name on the back of his shirt
playing up front for Tottenham.

"I remember a few times when people where openly giving me
abuse and I was only nine or ten. Oi kid he plays for Tottenham you
little prick! In retrospect getting regular abuse from random strangers
prepared me very well for Twitter."

Thankfully his namesake had left Spurs by January 1998 when Bob
Wilson took him and a group of school friends on a little match day
stadium tour in for his 10thbirthday. A fully kitted Tom Rosenthal was
given a tour which included a quick visit to the changing rooms where
Bob, the Goalkeeping Coach, introduced him to David Seaman. Quite

Rosenthal and friends at the Barca Fan Park pre-match

a special day for a young lad; *"He put his hand over my face and it covered the entirety of my head."* As he recalls the Arsenal won that day with 2 goals from Marc Overmars. It was the fourth game in a 19 match unbeaten run that was to take the Gunners to their first title in 9 years and his first as a fan.

CHAMPIONS LEAGUE... WEMBLEY DINNERS AND AWAY DAYS

Rosenthal's memories of the Champions League feature some classic away days (beyond the near shitting in a bag evening), but his earliest recollections oddly feature themed meals.

When Arsenal spent two seasons playing their home games in the competition at Wembley, Rosenthal's dad was always working on the matches for ITV. Therefore in the season after he has seen Wenger bring a league and FA Cup Double to Highbury he found himself a regular for the following two seasons in what was called the 'Champions Club' at Wembley. It was essentially the area of the stadium where all the sponsors and advertisers would entertain their corporate clients and he vividly remembers that the meal served up pre-match was based on the cuisine of the visiting club's country.

So a lovely pasta dish, when Fiorentina came to town or indeed special paella when the Catalan giants arrived is recalled with some affection. When AIK Solna were the visitors the dinner was Swedish meatballs but as Rosenthal's looks back the way he saw it at that age, it was a case of the worse the food the better Arsenal's chances of winning the ensuing game.

"Shit meals generally meant shit teams. If an eastern European team turned up yeah you had some awful goulash mess but you thought at least we're probably on for three points."

A year later his favourite Champions League away day was the trip to AC Milan in 2008 where a Cesc Fabregas inspired Arsenal became the only English team to have won in the San Siro against both Milan giants. Although both goals came late in the game, to Rosenthal's recollection Arsenal completely outplayed their illustrious opponents and were simply sensational that evening. It was his first visit to the magnificent stadium but he was up in the Gods and so far from the pitch that night, which strangely added to the occasion.

"We were so far away from the pitch in the San Siro that when Fabregas shot for his goal it seemed like it took a minute to go in. It was incredible but from so high up in the stands it took a while to actually realise what had happened."

Although the occasion did not end well for Arsenal he loved the trip to the Camp Nou in 2011 when van Persie was sent off. Another night where injustice could have caused searing anger, but all he can remember are the Arsenal fans repeatedly singing the Alex Song ditty to the tune of 'Up Where We Belong'

For those who haven't had the pleasure.
Alex Dimitri Song-Billong
He plays the holding role
Scores the occasional goal
Alex Dmitri Song-Billong
He's number seventeen
He is our midfield screen

THE ARSENAL FLAT

Home for Rosenthal is an Islington flat shared with his lifelong best mate who is also a Gooner. The lads' pad is a stroll to the Emirates where they sit in the North Upper with a few ex university friends all of whom have stayed in touch through the shared passion for Arsenal.

He is proud that one main wall and even some of the domestic appliances have been 'Arsenalised'. They only do them of the star players these days, but back in the day, the club shop used to stick postcard sized player pictures with the autographs on. They would buy selections of these photos and cover the wall, quite often opting for the obscure fringe payers or the up and coming talents. These were all placed randomly on the 'Arsenal wall of fame'.

There is or has been Mart Poom, Frimpong, a young Francis Coquelin, Wenger, Gallas, Rosicky, a Diaby, a Fabregas and many more. If players leave, well their pictures remain smiling at the room, but if they leave badly like Gallas or Fabregas their pictures remain for a long while, not removed but reversed, so like the naughty school boy they are sent to face the wall. Rosenthal adds that Ian Wright is on the fridge and Aaron Ramsey on the tumble dryer.

THROWN OUT OF THE LANE FOR MUGGING OFF A TOTTENHAM MULLET

It may be case of saving the best, or certainly the funniest until last, because Rosenthal thinks that in hindsight perhaps his funniest Arsenal related was at White Hart Lane in 2007.

Because of getting tickets via his dad for away matches when younger, he has quite often been in sort of 'supposed' neutral areas. One such occasion was in 2007/8 when Arsenal beat the old enemy 3-1 at their place and Rosenthal and a few friends were in what they believed to be a 'technically' neutral corporate area. However he was 19 and found it, shall we say, hard to contain his emotion back then.

"So I was generally being obnoxious, and I have no excuse for it. There were some Tottenham fans in front of me and they were mouthing off but there was this one particular guy who had an awful mullet haircut and was giving it large and got my back up. So when we equalised I did something terrible and gave this guy's mullet a sly little tug."

He somehow managed to avoid a slap and with a Jose Reyes like protestation of innocence, but obviously his card was marked. Then the second Arsenal goal, a screamer from Fabregas went in on the 80th minute, and, lesson not learned, he celebrated a little too vociferously in this area that he thought was supposed to be neutral. At that point, with the game turning against the home team, it dawned on Rosenthal and his friends that his dad had indeed got them tickets, not in a neutral stand but a Tottenham one.

Mullet was turning round having a go and it was firmly time to get their heads down but it was too late. Chewing gum and lighters began flying in his direction and shouts of 'Oi there are Gooners in here!' The next thing he knew was that a steward had arrived and, having singled him out as the most inflammatory, was bundling him out of the stand. Then this steward basically just told him to get out of the stadium.

"So I had to leave White Hart Lane by myself but the guys around me, including mullet bloke, were threatening to follow me out and find me to kick my head in, quite rightly to be fair because I had been so obnoxious. I left via the concourse and as I did I turned around to see one skinhead Tottenham fan punching a wall in frustration which I still believe to be the greatest thing I have ever witnessed."

It was a 'Spur' of the moment thing but on finding himself escorted out and then left alone, he felt he had to seek immediate refuge. At only 19, Rosenthal, on his own with his pals still inside, was not about to wait and see if the Mullet and his cronies were hot on his heels.

As luck would have it directly opposite there was a church which was in the middle of hosting a Nigerian wedding. He ran across the road into the church garden as the guests went in, and hid crouching behind a bush.

"Let's just say as a panting terrified white boy it became swiftly apparent I didn't really belong on either side of the wedding. But the bride and groom were just coming out of the entrance and nobody wanted to wreck the photos so they just kept on throwing confetti as I cowered in the background in a hedge."

From his protected vantage point he was able to study the exit from which he had been evicted to ensure none of the irate Spurs fans had made good on their promise. When he was sure that they hadn't, probably hoping their team might equalise he managed with his corporate pass to get to the hospitality area. The whole terrifying experience must have only lasted 10 minutes, although it seemed longer to him at the time, because he arrived back into the lounge just in time to see Adebayor score a spectacular volley, the third and clinching goal in the 93rd minute.

"So the lesson to be learnt is there is no neutral stand at the North London Derby and don't celebrate when you are in a Tottenham stand. Also always keep an eye out for a Tottenham fan punching a wall, it really is great stuff to witness."

It was the same year that Tom had met Arsene Wenger on an Arsenal away trip to Fratton Park. When his dad introduced him, Arsene said 'ah, you are the clever one I hear', remarkably remembering a previous conversation where his father had mentioned he was studying philosophy at university.

Are clever philosophy students generally obnoxious enough to get themselves thrown out of White Hart Lane for mouthing off at the North London Derby? I wonder how many mullets Aristotle sneakily pulled in his time?

AN ARSENAL RAMBLE WITH JIM CAMPBELL

J im Campbell may well just be the next big thing on the observational stand-up circuit, but he is also one quarter of the biggest and funniest football podcasts 'The Football Ramble'. Too many purely Arsenal podcasts are made of Gooners trying to be funny but the Ramble is made of four comedians who do it effortlessly. Given the huge success of the Football Ramble, Campbell has well-articulated and strong views on the new rise of alternative football media but more of that to come. Firstly how does a comedian residing in Brighton who spends much of his time on stage talking about growing up on the mean streets of Rainham, Essex, find his football ties in the better half of North London?

FROM WRIGHTY TO SEAMAN

For Campbell the answer is instant and straight forward, *"I can lay all the blame at the feet of Ian Wright."*. No one in his immediate family was a football fan so there was no domestic influence or guidance. He grew up in Rainham and virtually everyone there supported West Ham. Whilst there may have been a sprinkling of Arsenal or Tottenham rebels at his school it was firmly a claret and blue area. *"I have an uncle who is a West Ham fan, who tried to indoctrinate me as a kid. In fact he took me to Upton Park and was very disappointed when I bought an Arsenal badge on the way home. I just liked Arsenal more."*

At the time he first recalled being really into Arsenal it was because of Merson and Wrighty. It was a team built on the solid back four and a workman like midfield. They were dour to watch much of the time but then there was the *'Magic Man'* and the *'Goal Machine'*.

"I had probably missed the best of the George Graham teams as my awakening came around the time of the domestic Cup double in 1993. In fact the League Cup with the brilliant Merson goal and then poor old Steve Morrow falling off Adams' shoulders."

"But so much of it for me was about Ian Wright. It's that bizarre thing you do as a kid when you are playing with your mates you pick a player to be and I was always Wrighty. Something about the way he played the game; he was fast, always had a smile on his face and you could see how much he was enjoying it. He was like a fan on the *pitch and he absolutely was that because he was such a late developer. Everything about him was so infectious to me back then and of course he scored a hell of a lot of goals."*

He recalls with Wrighty though that it was not just the amount of goals but also the wonderful variety of them. Long range screamers, short range poached ones, left footed, right footed, headers and volleys. Most importantly for Arsenal at that time, as Campbell recalls, Wrighty was the man who would get his team out of a hole. In the same way Lineker was for England, Ian Wright was that guy for Arsenal. You just knew as a fan that they were going to get you a goal.

As he grew up Campbell stopped pretending to be a primary school Ian Wright. The reality of his lack of actual footballing ability superseded his desire to run about in the park doing a bad impression of his idol. As often happens to the lad who is not very good on pitch and is one of the last picked by the two captains, he ends up between the sticks. That lad was Jim Campbell, so in his senior school years the new hero was David Seaman.

"I used to love Seaman as well because later on I was often in goal. Just in the park; headers and volleys, jumpers for goalposts stuff. I did not realise how brave this probably was at the time, but I loved him so much I used to walk around Essex in a goal keeper's shirt with Seaman to the back. It was a bit sad at the end with the ponytail and his midlife crisis on the pitch. I still loved him but honestly David you may as well have come out of the tunnel on a Harley Davidson!"

When George Graham left, so much changed and as a teenager watching from a far there was so much to admire and get excited about. There were so many players to fall in love with and to inspire a young fan beyond occasional relief from the tedium provided by Merson and Wright at the back end of Graham's tenure.

BERGKAMP AND HENRY

Campbell, like most of us, is happy to debate which of Bergkamp and Henry deserves the greatest tag. He suggests that perhaps of the two, most fans might select Bergkamp because his arrival changed so much at Arsenal. Some of the goals and equally the assists were ingenious and wonderfully crafted. He finds himself watching them over and over even now and often still scratching his head in disbelief.

"Like the famous Newcastle one. I believe he meant it but no matter how many times I watch it I still don't know understand how he did it!

One of the best things about Dennis is that he said after he retired that he never scored his perfect goal. He had an idea of the perfect goal he wanted to score but he never managed to pull it off. How good must that goal in his head be to be better than the one at St James Park? I love that about him, perfectionist."

Henry edges it though for Campbell. *"For me Henry though was like a superhero. He did things that were just obscene."*

His personal favourite was the goal Henry scored at Stamford Bridge which was as much about his intelligence and ingenuity; ironically as he recalls it came from a very un-Arsenal type ball over the top from Vieira. I would encourage you to Google it if you cannot recall it, from a 2-2 draw in March 2003. Here is Campbell's recollection followed by the summation from the man on Sky Sports that day:

"It came over the top and Henry was closing in on Cudicini, he barely got a toe to the ball and it seemed a simple claim for the keeper but somehow Henry got there and swivelled his body turning the hapless Cudicini and he just tapped it in to the empty net. The finesse was unbelievable."

'That's the measure of the man. You think you have him under control and then he responds like that. Finishing of the highest quality!'"

Another Henry moment was the Liverpool game in the unbeaten season, where having gone out of the Champions League and the FA Cup in a week, the whole season was in the balance. We were 2-1 down and then Henry just happened; leaving Carragher on his arse and the whole Liverpool defence as statues.

"For it to be such a specific moment in that season and for it to be defined by the brilliance of one man. Just wow! That sort of stuff is what I mean when I say he was like a superhero, more than a normal human to be revered."

Another favourite Henry moment that just confirmed his legend status was the comeback goal against Leeds in the FA Cup. What made it even more special for Campbell, beyond the occasion and the reaction which we all talk about to this day and will do for years to come, was the almost perfect symmetry of the type of goal it was and that it had the Henry hallmark. He came back after a long time away and what he did instantly, mirrored what he had always done.

"The great thing was that it was his signature goal. There is the Cruyff turn and there is the Henry goal. How often do you hear commentators saying 'that was Henryesque' or 'there was a touch of Henry about that finish'? So basically everyone in the stadium, in the

commentary box and on the pitch knew what he was going to do, he even pointed to where he wanted the ball from Song and still they were unable to stop it."

APPRECIATING THE MEMORIES

The early Wenger years have given Arsenal fans so many fabulous memories, an exhilarating brand of football and some stellar football-ers. Campbell feels that sometimes our supporters need to bring this to mind to aid perspective in the poor seasons.

When Campbell fell in love with Arsenal, if the idea of champagne football was far-fetched, the idea of big name foreign stars was unthink-able. The arrival of Bergkamp was to signify a change though, because whilst Arsenal had signed foreign players who they hoped would be stars, Dennis was one. The next arrival to truly fire the fans' imagination was Marc Overmars and what a difference he was to make in his first season. He feels that perhaps younger fans today, for whom it is the norm, may not realise just how incredible it was to see these types of players coming first to your league and then amazingly to your own club.

"In the late 90s to have such established world renowned players at your club just seemed so impossibly glamorous. It was like if you were directing the school play and Michael Fassbender had agreed to be in it. It just seemed ridiculous that these players would be playing for my club."

Although not a huge name to English fans when Wenger signed him, Manu Petit was to be a World Cup Winner with Vieira, his Arsenal midfield partner, only 10 months later. The arrival of Petit and Over-mars were the vital ingredients which turned the Gunners into Cham-pions again. Campbell succinctly summarised in one sentence, quite brilliantly, the impact of the two on the Gunners back then.

"Overmars and Petit I guess were the players that I wanted and we had all hoped Stefan Schwarz and Glen Helder would be!"

It is the very fact that we have seen the teams of 97/98, 01/02 and 03/04 that makes us Gooners so lucky in Campbell's mind. You have to keep the brilliance of what you have seen and keep thinking of Robert Pires in full flow because others cannot. Most fans won't ever experi-ence what Arsenal fans have experienced, especially going a domestic league season unbeaten. Even if they do they are only going to be join-ing a tiny elite club and be matching the feat of the first team to have done it in the modern era.

"There are so many incredible memories that are beyond the actual winning of things. It is the style in which we won them that you can truly savour. It is not like we blunted our way to these titles. It is better to have won a league and lost than never to have won a league at all I say."

Looking back with fondness, as we all do, on the 2003/4 season we should mention that it was also the season that saw Campbell's first visit to Highbury. I am not saying he is unlucky but we only lost 4 games in that season and he managed to be at one of them. Not only that, but in January of 2004 we played Middlesbrough three times at home in a 15 day period. We beat them twice convincingly 4-1, first in the Premier League on the 10th of January and again in the FA Cup on the 24th. Sandwiched in the middle of these two emphatic victories was the first leg of the League Cup Semi-Final, which we contrived to lose with a second string team by a solitary goal. Campbell still loved it and recalls that Highbury felt smaller to be in than it has looked to him on the television and recalls with quirky pride that he saw David Bentley play for the Gunners!

Since the first pilgrimage in 2004, Campbell gets to the Arsenal as often as he can when his comedy commitments and Football Ramble schedule allows.

THE FOOTBALL RAMBLE, PODS AND BLOGS

'The Football Ramble' is the largest independent podcast in the UK and one of the largest anywhere in the world. It has been running since 2007 and we can safely say it was ahead of its time in many senses, but it continues to evolve, in what is an ever competitive space. Podcasts are undoubtedly, along with blogging, a modern day phenomenon. This is true in many walks of life, but perhaps none more so than when it comes to football. Given that Campbell is at the vanguard, certainly of the football pod, his views on it are fascinating and insightful.

Campbell agrees that the Arsenal blog and podcast world is indeed swamped. However he likes this because more than any other club, probably only Liverpool and Man United have similar, Arsenal basically have their own fan media and it's away from the official Arsenal channels. He would visit Arseblog for the Arsenal news rather than go to the official Arsenal site because for him it is more reliable. *"Not only that it's more interesting, it's funny and has more of a human face to it."*

"I think it is fascinating the way it is going to evolve. I have been a guest on Arsecast and of course I co-host the Football Ramble and for me it's the modern equivalent of the terraces. The idea of your team being supported by a group of guys who live nearby and who represent you is long gone. Now the fans in the stadia, certainly in the Premier League, are the minority effectively. This idea of having all these opinions floating around on blogs or pods, from those who are supporters of the club (wherever they may be from) rather than those with an agenda or associated with it or trying to get clicks for a media website, it fosters a sense of community. It gives you a truer picture of what the mood is fanwise."

The popularity of blogs and podcasts is fabulous because it has seen them become credible as a standalone medium, rather than just something that rivals the traditional media such as Sky Sports, BT Sports, the BBC and the mainstream. Campbell is convinced that the reason why the new media, of which he is proud to be a part, has one major advantage over the mainstream establishment.

"They can't acknowledge the fundamental truth that we all love about football, that it is ridiculous. It's a fucking ridiculous, big, absurd soap opera with teenage millionaires behaving terribly. I love that about it, it's a circus and they can't acknowledge that because they have to protect their product. They have to give it gravitas and yes it deserves that as well. It should be taken seriously in a lot of ways as well, but we need to be able to laugh at it and appreciated its silliness as well and that is where their alternative media has sprung up from. Because if we are honest we all love the silly side of the game that the traditional media won't touch and they can't because they are terrible at it when they try."

He does wonder where this growth in the 'alternative' media will end though because some of the blogs and pods are massive now and are here to stay. The individuals that run them are making a living out of it. That is a sea change and something that has only happened in the last two or three years. So these new media are not going anywhere and it will be fascinating to see how the traditional media react because at the moment when they try and replicate it, for Campbell at least, it does not work.

"Ex-pros they see the game in a different way from how we do and in a way it's not for them, it's not about them. It's almost we are talking about you not to you. Robbie Savage can't appreciate all the things we think about Robbie Savage because he is too close to it. He is trapped

No football material at Edinburgh 2014

being Robbie Savage which is a fate I would not wish on anyone, apart from Robbie Savage, of course!"

Campbell and the Football Ramble Pod team have been fortunate enough to travel to the last Euros in the Ukraine and the 2010 World Cup in South Africa. Their trips have been largely self-funded, although *"we were sponsored incredibly, by Paco Rabanne to go to the World Cup, which if you smelled any of us, you would know is absurd!"* They did some stuff for their sponsor's website and did several live World Cup themed pods. Sadly they did not actually make it into any games but given how shocking England were that was no great loss. Just being out there for the party was a memorable experience.

They did their thing in the Ukraine in 2012 and did manage to get to the England win over Sweden. What Campbell recalls most clearly was the double celebration awarded to now Gunner Danny Welbeck's goal. *"What I remember most was we celebrated Danny Welbeck's goal, then saw it on the big screen, realised it was this smart little tidy back heel that he meant and went mental celebrating all over again."*

Campbell and the Ramble team also spent some time with the famed England band, although he regrets not blunting their instruments.

"I hate the England band to be honest because they play the same old songs all the time and they are negative songs. The tone of the song is 'come on England do it against all the odds' and it grinds you down. We have been saying for a long time on the Football Ramble that they should do the Jurassic Park theme and let the fans sing 'Come on Engerland' to that. But will they fuck?"

FOOTBALL BANTER IN STAND UP

Campbell, like most of his peers, declines to use football material in his stand-up routine. The subject matter can divide a room and cause many to switch off.

"I did used to talk about how Wayne Rooney's brother was for a time employed as a Wayne Rooney lookalike, which is the most depressing thing I had ever heard. And even though that story which I make a joke of is not really about football, you still see some in the audience switch off when they hear the two words 'Wayne Rooney'."

In a sense it is a shame and he would like to do a show with just football banter and material. He believes The Football Ramble show proves there is comfortably enough material out there for an amusing show every week, but only for an exclusively football loving audience. He would love to do a show just on modern football, tackling it head on and perhaps endeavour to show those who don't like football to understand why so many do. To tell an audience how football at the top level is essentially this wonderful giant cartoon full of millionaire babies. There are so many anecdotes to relate and stories to tell.

"The best example is Mathieu Flamini. He has become a bit of a joke figure because he just points and kicks. Actually to be fair to him his pointing is indisputably world class, but this guy has patented an acid that may replace oil and save the planet from its dependency on fossil fuels. That is absurd, I love it. It is like Tony Stark for God's sake!" (That is Iron Man for non-Marvel geeks.)

SUPERSTITIONS AND JINXES

Campbell explains that over the years of supporting Arsenal, particularly in recent times, he has been conditioned to never be able to relax even if the team is two goals to the good. Even if the Gunners are two-nil up after 70 or 80 minutes he is still unable to relax and just enjoy the match. He will seldom allow himself to even utter the words 'I think we are going to win this' out loud for fear of jinxing his team, because we footy fans think like that. It is like in the old days continually refreshing Ceefax in the hope that the score you don't like will miraculously change.

An example of Campbell allowing himself to slip from his usual conditioned self is offered as proof of his ability to be a jinx. In April 2016 having done a Football Ramble live show in Newcastle, he was having lunch in a bar whilst watching the West Ham game. Campbell committed the school boy error of allowing himself a small fist pump under the table. Despite the low key nature of the premature display of over confidence, he knew immediately he had gone too far.

"I sort of knew I had done too much and they then scored two goals in a minute, went ahead and we scraped a 3-3. I sort of felt personally responsible, 350 miles away for allowing myself to be smug enough to think we were going to win the game because we were 2 nil up. I just feel like I have to be, not negative so much with Arsenal but ludicrously cautious or it will come back and bite me on the arse."

As I write that, I sort of know that so many football fans reading this will be nodding their heads and wondering whether or not to change their lucky boxers or shirt they have worn for the last few victories.

CUP WINNERS CUPS TRIUMPH AND DESPAIR

The 1994 and 1995 Cup Winners Cup campaigns fall firmly into the strong early recollections of Campbell. The 1994 win was special for all Arsenal fans and a huge triumph for the tactical acumen of George Graham. He misses the straight knock out competitions and there could be no argument about whether you deserved to win it (not sure what this means?). Arsenal that year played some top sides en route to Copenhagen. It seemed a wonderful adventure but he also felt Arsenal were learning how to play in Europe on the way.

"We hammered Standard Liege and Eddie McGoldrick played a blinder, not an expression you hear often. Kevin Campbell was in the team, which I obviously really enjoyed. Just having someone in your team with your surname scoring on a regular basis is a brilliant thing when you are a 12 year old!"

"Of course then beating Parma, a team no one expected us to beat, in the final, without Ian Wright. A team that had Tomas Brolin, when he was the size of a normal human, Faustino Asprilla and Gianfranco Zola all in the same attack. Our defence blunted their multi-talented

attack and at a time when Italian defences were the best in Europe we breached their back line with the wonderful goal from Smudger. The feeling of having won a European trophy the next day at school was absolutely amazing. I will never forget that feeling and I hope that another generation of Arsenal fans gets to experience that at some point."

Don't we all Jim, don't we all!!

Of course with the highs you have to experience the corresponding lows, and that came the following season in the same competition with Nayim from the halfway line. Campbell felt it particularly because of his personal affinity with David Seaman.

"With Nayim being ex Spurs, it was all so heartbreaking, but that's football isn't it? That was as gutted as I have ever been in my life actually, just devastated. I guess though it is with those losses more than the victories that you earn your stripes as a supporter. The suffering and the embarrassment and when other supporters laud it over you that's where you as a fan, put in your hours."

Conversely the next day in school after that defeat and the nature of it was about as horrible as the previous year had been wonderful.

EBOUE

In an enjoyable chat that had covered considerable ground, Campbell suddenly decided that he was supposed to be a comedian and should be funnier. To facilitate he suggested we talk about Emmanuel Eboue. Why not indeed?

He loved the character of the crazy Ivorian and in the run to the Champions League Final points out that he was magnificent marauding down the right. Much later when he had lost his regular right back berth to Sagna, there was that horrible instance when the Emirates crowd really turned on the player in a match against Wigan.

Eboue had come on for an injured Nasri and had a shocker, causing a very over the top reaction by the fans and Wenger then having to withdraw him. Ironically as Campbell recalls it was like the fans realised how much they had hurt the player and turned him into a cult hero.

"It was like the fans realised they had genuinely caused a human being some serious pain with the treatment he had got at the Emirates and it was great to see that someone somewhere within our crowd decided we should redress it. You only come to see Eboue was just a wonderful example of the best of football support."

Eboue was however always playing the clown both off and on the pitch, and was evidently extremely popular with his team mates. Campbell has a couple of personal favourite Eboue anecdotes. One of which you can find on Youtube, is from the 2010 World Cup when Ivory Coast played North Korea.

"A North Korean player was taking instruction from the manager while a player was getting treatment. Eboue was over there because I think he was waiting to take a throw and he was listening to this coach's instructions, nodding along as he was speaking, as if he understood Korean and was finding out the oppositions tactics. He was a clown but he was our clown and a lot of fun."

There's another story from 2006 when Gilberto Silva, who was captain in Thierry Henry's injury absence, decided to host a Christmas party for his players. Eboue arrived early dressed in a full tiger costume and proceeded to sit behind the sofa pouncing out in full roar every time a new team mate arrived.

Although clearly bonkers but not as bonkers as some....

THE LANDLADY OF THE LILLY LANGTRY

Campbell was a told a lovely story by a friend who had studied at the University of East Anglia in Norwich. His girlfriend at the time had worked behind the bar of a pub called the Lilly Langtry. On the outside it was a seemingly normal pub, but on the inside one of its bars was a full on shrine to none other than Jose Antonio Reyes.

Apparently the landlady had decided she should try and get into football a bit so he could chat to her regular punters when games were on. The problem was she only got as far as Reyes and decided that was enough for her. She became genuinely obsessed with Arsenal's Spanish hunk, but sadly for her it was about the time poor Jose was getting home sick and was getting loaned to Real Madrid.

Undaunted though the shrine building continued and the walls of the pub were covered with framed Arsenal, Seville and Madrid Reyes shirts and photos of her idol. She even had a full sized cardboard cutout of him behind the bar. She renamed the Golden Triangle Bar in her pub for her fixation.

As Campbell has already hinted he believes Thierry Henry to be a superhero, but he is not about to build a shrine for him in his bedroom. He is not sure his partner would appreciate it which is the strangest part of the above story.

"This woman ran the pub with her husband who apparently didn't seem to mind. For me that's as weird as the rest of it. What was going on there?"

It was wonderful discussing all things Arsenal and taking him on a journey through his love of all things football, but I will allow him to sum it up as he did it so well….

"The endlessness of it is what is so marvellous about it because there is always another game and another season. One of the brilliant things about Arsenal though, is when they do win things and they do achieve things it is like I'm in that moment I am 12 again when I first felt the joy of those moments like Copenhagen. The purest most satisfying feeling that comes with your team winning something and the crazy thing is that it is 'we' because you feel like you have achieved it too or with them. You and your mates have been validated in this thing you love for a year or a day even. It is mad isn't it how these moments make you feel."

A fitting end to this beautiful ramble with Jim Campbell.

HUGH DENNIS AKA JOHNNY COME LATELY

When it comes to comedy genres Hugh Dennis covers most of the bases. From stand-up to impressions and from sketch shows to sitcoms, this most likeable of performers had been ever present in our lives' through our screens since 1990. In the early 1990s primarily with his long time friend and collaborator Steve Punt on 'Canned Carrot' and then 'The Mary Whitehouse Experience' with Newman and Baddiel; whilst behind the scenes providing many of the voices for the Spitting Image puppets.

Since 2005 Dennis has been ever present on satirical news review panel show 'Mock the Week', whilst simultaneously using his finely honed improvisational skills in the hugely popular sitcom 'Outnumbered'. The latter show, in which he starred as long suffering history teacher and father of three, Pete Brockman, became more successful year on year. The 4th series in 2011 won Best Comedy at the National Television Award and the last time we saw the Brockmans on Christmas Eve 2014 they pulled in close to £10 million viewers.

JOHNNY COME LATELY

So why, for a man so much in the public eye, is it rarely if ever, mentioned that Dennis is an Arsenal fan? It was an obvious place to start any interview, particularly when the interview is about being a Gooner. So was it parents, school, friends?

The answer is none of the above and the truth is that Dennis spent far too many years doing one of his best impressions; that of a boy, then a teenager and latterly a grown man, loving the game yet supporting no team. It is a sorry tale of excuses; absurdities and denial so

if you are of an angry or nervous disposition perhaps skip the next few pathetic pages!

Although born in Northampton, his family moved to the Isle of Dogs when Dennis was infant school age. His father, now a Bishop, was the Vicar of the Isle of Dogs. The Isle, as Dennis describes it, is where Millwall should be but isn't and is firmly in the middle of Millwall and West Ham country. He and his brother, parachuted in with the new vicar, were quite obviously the only middle class kids in a very working class mid 1960s Isle of Dogs. The siblings learned very swiftly that they were different and found themselves regularly stopped in the street by big and scary lads, who always had the same 'polite' question to ask – Are you West Ham or Millwall?

"When you saw big lads coming towards you in the distance you had to try and decide are they West Ham or Millwall? If I give the

wrong answer you were a dead man. So weirdly because of this constant threat I sort of decided not to support anyone."

Despite this, by the age of five, Dennis was already completely in love with football. His best friend at his school was a huge West Ham fan, so to follow suit would have been easy but at that young age he made a decision that he was not going to support anyone at all and was just going to play instead, whenever he could.

Now looking back he is not even totally certain it was a conscious decision but he does know it was sort of ludicrous because football has formed the architecture of his life. Having moved on to primary school in a new parish for his dad, in Smithfield in the City of London, he still maintained his support abstention. Even though he was addicted to watching football all the time, such as 'On the Ball' and 'The Big Match' and the self-preservation validation was no longer an excuse.

"It was totally bonkers because by the time I was at my first junior school in Smithfield everyone at the school was a Gooner. In my secondary school everyone was a Gooner or supported Spurs. Yet still I maintained this 'I don't support any one I just play!'"

In 1969 Dennis was taken to Highbury for the first time and this experience, in his mind, might have been another reason for not admitting to his support. His first professional match was at Arsenal for a school friend's birthday treat. He recalls his Arsenal mad chum must have been so desperate to go to Highbury because the chosen match was Arsenal Reserves versus Swindon Town Reserves on a school night.

"It was freezing cold, it was foggy and it was Swindon and I think that made me feel even more that perhaps playing rather than watching football was for me."

The two teams were kicking lumps out of each other. Dennis reflects that it was probably a grudge match. Because even though Swindon had beaten Arsenal in the previous season's League Cup Final, Arsenal had taken their place in the Inter-City Fairs Cup, as only Division One or top flight teams were allowed in. Of course the Gunners went on to win that European competition, that they only got into by default, and breaking their 17 year trophy drought.

So glory beckoned for Arsenal and it was to follow the next season with a League and Cup Double and whilst Dennis knew all the players and watched the triumph with interest, he still never admitted to himself or anyone else that he supported them.

This self-denial continued through senior school and through university even though Dennis continued to be obsessed with watching and more importantly playing football, captaining virtually every school and college team he represented. He always felt he was playing to a high standard, primarily as a graceful central defender. One of his proudest achievements was as a sixth-former to lead as captain, his school UCS Hampstead, to the finals of the Public Schools Cup.

"You might think all the public schools play Rugby but all the oldest and most established like Eton and Winchester play football because it pre dates Rugger. The thing that was very weird was that because it was public schools it was the 'National Public Schools 6 Aside Cup!' Have you ever heard of 6 aside football for 6th formers?

His reached the final and he made the mistake that allowed Oldham Grammar School to win 1-0. He was nut-megged on the edge of the penalty area and was crestfallen. He got his losers medal from a guy called Sammy Chung, who had been the manager of Wolves. He had witnessed the terrible mistake and had a look of sympathy in his eye as he placed the medal that Dennis did not even want, around his neck.

Yet the pattern of playing the game whilst watching any football he could with no allegiance was to continue through Cambridge University, where he was to meet his chief collaborator and close friend Steve Punt. Both had joined the Cambridge Footlights and began writing and performing with Nick Hancock. You would have thought that spending many years working closely at university and beyond with a football crazy Stoke City nut in Hancock, might have made Dennis see the light.

Surely buying his first house in 1990 just off Upper Street in Islington on the route of the Arsenal celebratory open top bus tour was the moment Dennis' eyes would be opened; opened to the deeper joy of watching football with passion and with a vested interest. This was after all the year, after the most incredible end to a season in the history of English football, which he had watched and enjoyed.

"I lived in an area that was all Arsenal. I bought it in 1990 right after Anfield 89 and I was still maintaining my inexplicable stance."

In 1992 a group of predominantly North London dwelling comedians and writers had grouped together to play football every Tuesday evening. The venue Highbury and the playing surface, astonishingly, was actually the hallowed turf. Yes, Dennis and peers such as Patrick Marber, Angus Deaton, David Baddiel and Clive Anderson were all part of the original group of about 25 and now 24 years later they still play every Tuesday. The venue is now the 'Arsenal in the Community Hub' and some of the faces have changed. Clive Anderson still plays in his 60s; although according to Dennis he does not move about that much,

Hugh in five-a-side action for Comic Relief

more standing in the centre circle, like a celebrity version of a latter day Jan Molby.

"It was absolutely fantastic as you used to drive into Highbury on a Tuesday night and the doorman would say 'good evening sir' and you went to the proper dressing room and on to the real pitch. This of course makes the whole not supporting Arsenal thing even madder, what was I thinking?"

In March 1997 in the season Arsene Wenger has arrived, Dennis's son, Fred, was born. He was given a miniature Arsenal shirt by a close friend, Macca. It was this event and the fact that he had just started playing football at Highbury that finally got Dennis questioning his almost lifelong 'Gooner denial'.

FINALLY...

"So I guess I finally admitted it to myself and declared myself a Gooner for real in about 2000. I loved watching football so despite not actually being a fan for the 1998 double, I was acutely aware of the team and had watched it all."

The reality was that whilst Dennis has always been addicted to playing and watching football he was also a connoisseur of football. He had always admired slick, passing and beautiful football and hated what he describes as 'hoof it' football. He had much enjoyed the West Ham style he watched in the 1960s as a boy. Therefore it was the realisation that the new brand of football Arsene Wenger had introduced at Highbury was exactly the fantastic style he wanted to watch.

Now as a proud holder of two season tickets in the West Upper and a regular since 2000 he is highly embarrassed at his weird story and odd journey. He looks back and admits now to being ashamed that he could have supported Arsenal since he was in primary school and on so many occasions subsequently, but failed to do so. He confesses to asking himself if he can now call himself a real fan having only been one for 16 years.

'I know I am though because once you have decided of course, it completely takes over your life, right down to the purchase of Arsenal Deodorant from the club shop."

Dennis is quick to point out that since his declaration that he was indeed a Gooner, the team have not once failed to reach the knockout phases of the European Champions League. Coincidence?

TALKING ARSENAL AND 60,000 EXPERTS WHO LOVE A GEGEN PRESS!

Despite his late arrival to the now all enveloping Arsenal addiction, for Hugh Dennis there has always been the addiction of watching the wider game. So much so that until five years ago, for his own sanity and his marriage, he refused to allow himself Sky Sports. He knew that once it was in the house he would quite literally watch any football that was on if he was not working. That has indeed proved to be the case. The football addiction extends, as it does for most of us, to talking about the game and over a pint in a favourite pub preferably.

Excuses and opportunities for such chats are not hard to find in his average working week. The Arsenal contingent on *Mock the Week* regularly delay filming discussing what is happening in N5, more often than not what is going wrong. A huge amount of his time is spent doing voice overs and these are virtually all done in Soho and most of Soho is Red and White it seems.

Dennis famously does impressionistic voiceovers for video clips on *Mock the Week* and his work on the film of Wenger and Thierry Henry presenting the Arsenal team to the Queen is the stuff of legend. If you have never seen this just use your search engine typing in 'Arsenal Meet the Queen (*Mock the Week*)'. Where else would Thierry introducing Denilson as a Brazilian gain the response from Her Majesty, 'Oh I like Brazilian myself but Phillip prefers a welcome mat.'?

Sadly he has not had an occasion to meet Wenger or work at any Arsenal functions. He observes with no bitterness and with a grin that Clive Anderson, Alan Davies and Dara O'Briain seem to have the monopoly on the Arsenal gigs.

"I think they must have heard I am a Johnny come lately."

Watching football and chatting about Arsenal he enjoys, but going to watch the team live at the Emirates he absolutely loves. He goes with his son and whilst obviously in the main enjoying the football, one facet of the match day experience that he particularly enjoys is the comedy value of the crowd. The fact that he is surrounded by 60,000 people, all of whom think they know an enormous amount about football, gives him singular pleasure. He simply loves hearing the constant stream of expert opinions and shall we say 'heart-felt advice' offered to the Arsenal players!

"There is a group of guys you just can hear where I sit; it is absolutely amazing that they cannot see the positives in anything. They use a collection of phrases they have picked up or learned. 'They've got to press higher up the pitch; No one is leaving their foot in, are they? You've got to put your foot in not leave it in! We are playing too high a line, just compress the pitch, and get it out wide!"

He loves going to the Emirates for the amusement provided by the fans as much as the football in a way; it is part of the entertainment to him because for him none of them truly have the knowledge. He explains that with pundits like Dixon or Carragher, when they explain why a player should or should not have done something, you know they know because they have been there and done it at the highest level. Whereas he feels even when playing he is still indecisive because he doesn't actually know the best thing to do half the time. *"In my opinion you have to know an awful lot about football to know anything about football."*

He contends that even five years ago no one had even heard of 'pressing a high line' let alone 'gegenpressing' and yet today fans use the phrases with abandon. He delights in hearing fans in the ground and fans debating on radio phone-ins liberally throwing out observations such as 'Well I think they should have used gegenpressing against that opposition' or 'they used a gegenpress, when they should have left a man in the hole!' Dennis enjoys listening to two fans debating and blinding each other with football jargon, safe in the knowledge that for the most part they are talking nonsense, but nonsense he loves listening to.

Whilst relishing everything about the Emirates match day, he is also quick to acknowledge that perhaps Arsenal fans, largely due to may being priced out over the years, do not generate the atmosphere others seem to manage. He ponders whether at Arsenal there may be an identity crisis, which may indeed be present at most larger successful clubs not still crucial to their community. He contrasts Arsenal to Portsmouth, where he has spent some time as both of his children were at Portsmouth Grammar School; and has a home on the South Downs. He is weirdly fond of Pompey and he thinks it is their strong sense of identity which was described to him once by the school head teacher. 'Portsmouth is like a northern town on the south coast.'

Dennis explains if you live in the South East of England nobody says *"I am Guildford till I die or I am Basingstoke till I die, but Pompey till I die sounds perfectly reasonable."*

This identity and mentality rubs off on the football club and Pompey fans. They have John Westwood, or Pompey Chime, who Dennis has met and interviewed, who has 62 Portsmouth FC tattoos, PFC engraved in his teeth, goes to every game bare-chested with a huge hat and a drum, while Arsenal have authors like Nick Hornby and middle aged comedians.

"Our fans have a certain reputation shall we say. You are, despite my earlier observations, as likely to overhear a conversation about ciabatta and olives as you are about gegenpressing or playing a high line."

A last observation from Dennis on matches is that he has decided that in recent seasons the Sunday late kick-offs are his favourite weekend games with 36 hours to relax first. He jokes *"the reason I like those so much is that you get the reset of the weekend to enjoy before the sense of disappointment sets in."*

THE ARSENAL WAY

Dennis, like many of us, finds himself contemplating life at Arsenal beyond Arsene Wenger. Again, like many he would love to see Bergkamp involved in some capacity. He does also acknowledge that *"Skyping his team talk into the dressing room on away nights might not be ideal."* He describes the Dutchman as the most intelligent footballer he has watched. The football Wenger introduced in the later 90s that convinced Hugh 'Johnny Come Lately' Dennis, to finally come off the fence had Bergkamp at the centre of it. He was integral to the new way the Frenchman wanted Arsenal to play and when he thinks of Bergkamp he is always reminded of Bobby Moore. In the 1960s when England World Cup winning captain was asked what makes a great footballer, his answer was along the lines of 'you have to know when someone is going to pass the ball to you and what you are going to do with it before they have'. That was Bergkamp all over and he cites the wonder goal against Newcastle as the perfect evidence of the advanced thinking of the Dutchman.

Growing up he reflects it was always said that Tottenham and West Ham both had a style of play and a philosophy associated to them. Arsenal of the 1960s, 70s and 80s had not really claimed or earned such an identity or perceived identity. Even the great 1971 Double winning team was functional and effective but had no style or particular panache. Since Arsene Wenger most football fans, even those that are loath to, have to admit that since 1997/98 Arsenal do have an attractive style of play firmly associated with them. For Hugh Dennis, the self-proclaimed 'Johnny Come Lately' of Arsenal celebrity fans and for thousands of Gooners around the globe, this is the question that keeps him awake at night (although not literally).

"I wonder that whoever finally comes in to replace Wenger, whether the club and we the fans will insist on the same style we have all become accustomed to."

Time will tell Hugh, time will tell.

MATT LUCAS, LITTLE BRITAIN'S BIGGEST GOONER

From his earliest mainstream comedy creation, George Dawes, in "Shooting Stars" to his worldwide success with then writing and performing partner David Walliams in "Little Britain", Matt Lucas has been creating hilarious and original characters, and with them catchphrases for over 20 years. A whole generation will find themselves using 'yeah but no but' or 'I want that one' fully aware that they have Lucas' genius creations Vicky Pollard and Andy Pipkin to thank. Now residing in America and forging a successful acting career in Hollywood as well as back home, Lucas is very much still one of the UK's most loved entertainers. He feels honoured to be working with the likes of Johnny Depp and Tim Burton, but I wonder if it is not they that are fortunate to have him in their version of Wonderland.

Lucas, soon to be back on our screens in Doctor Who, is certainly one of Arsenal's highest profile fans. He is still a regular visitor to the Emirates whenever work calls him back to the UK and whilst at his LA home he still rarely misses a match even at the most inconvenient of times. During what he described as his 'mercurial phase' at the peak of Little Britain's success, he had a box at the stadium. It was a case as he puts it, of if you could why wouldn't you, but that is not the type of fan Lucas is having been a match going fan since the early 1980s. So where did it begin with the Gunners for Lucas born in West London in 1974?

photo courtesy of Stuart Macfarlane and Arsenal FC

Matt Lucas is a Gooner!

It would be simple to say the love of Arsenal for him and his elder brother by 3 years was inherited from his father but the story behind his dad John's support deserves telling. In 1958 Lucas's late father who was then 14 had an awful bicycle accident that saw him catapulted at high speed over this own handle bars after colliding with a car. The injuries he sustained were sufficiently serious to see the teenage John Lucas require surgery. The surgeon, as it transpired, was also Arsenal's club doctor. At the time of the accident John Lucas was more of a cricket fan and if truth be told held little interest for the beautiful game. This was to change during the full year of recovery and rehabilitation because the kindly Arsenal affiliated surgeon used to give the brave youngster Highbury match tickets as a treat.

"So at the end of the 1950s, through adversity, my father was converted to football and discovered the joy of going to Highbury and a passion for the Arsenal. In due course this was passed down to my older brother and to me."

EARLY FOOTBALL EXPERIENCES

His father began taking a young Matt, aged six, to football but it would be fair to say at that age he had not grasped it. He recalls coming home from a friend's birthday party in May of 1980, to find his father and brother distraught but not truly grasping why. Ironically it was West Ham's reward for beating Arsenal at Wembley that was to be Lucas' first football match. His father took him and his brother to the Charity Shield between West Ham and Liverpool at the start of the 1980/81 season.

"I had a red and white teddy bear that I had been given; I was obsessed with teddies, so I supported Liverpool as they were in red. I remember feeling very unsettled and claustrophobic because we were behind fences and I had not really seen that on the TV. Even at that age I found that really dehumanizing and was very upset."

During that season he was occasionally taken, with his brother, to Highbury. He still struggled to relate to the action on the pitch and from his seat in the stands it all seemed so far away. There were no big screen action replays back then and at aged 6 it all seemed so distant and boring. However his ability to grasp the finer points of the game as it transpired did not impact his enjoyment.

"I was bored by the football but absolutely loved the occasion of it. Being taken by my dad who worked hard all week, with my brother, was a real treat."

A few years later, when Lucas was ten, his parents were to split up and the time spent at Highbury, with his father became increasingly important to him. By then Lucas was a real fan and was relishing the football, the team and not just the occasion. The penny had dropped when he was able to recognise and reacted to the players in red and white, as well as their opposition and for this he credits Panini!

PANINI FOOTBALL STICKERS

Even before being taken to Highbury and after it, Lucas recollects Sunday afternoons watching *The Big Match* and not enjoying or understanding the obvious pleasure derived by his father and brother. He would be sitting waiting for the amusing adverts which he did relate to. Again, as with the Highbury visits, it was the inclusion and the family closeness that he looked forward to not the action or the results which he did not understand.

It was not until he thinks the 1982/83 season that his relationship with football changed and the credit he lays firmly with his discovery and collection of Panini Stickers. The collecting (and so many will relate to this) became quickly obsessive. By then he was of an age where he was allowed to eagerly ride, from his house in Stanmore, to the Newsagents by Canons Park Station. With his 15 or 20 pence pocket money, he would buy the packet. Could he resist opening them in the shop and wait until he arrived home? Sometimes he managed it before carefully tearing open the small envelope. Two days later he would be swapping stickers with school friends, but something had changed.

"Suddenly I found I was watching The Big Match knowing who the players were. I would see and hear the commentators say Brian Talbot or Alan Sunderland and I would know them and things about them. Important information like the number of appearances they had made for the club up until the start of that season and how many goals they had scored. I would know who they had played for previously and if they had played for England or another country at full of U21 level."

The information in the Panini album and on the back of the sticker before Lucas peeled it off was educating him. His appreciation of football on the television and when he returned to Highbury as 1982/83 progressed had grown because Panini has given him context.

EARLY HIGHBURY RECOLLECTIONS

Newly armed with footballer stats and knowledge, Lucas was able to appreciate the trips to Highbury more. However until he was a teenager, the Saturday Arsenal experience was still more about the quality time with his brother and more particularly with his dad. Some of the vivid memories are quite random, but occasions where large crowd movements left a young terrified Lucas fearing for his life, still leave a scar. Matches where the visitors were Everton and Man United still haunt him to this day and the thoughts of terraces do not cause Lucas to hanker for the good old days.

One stand out memory that still makes him smile was a match when they, he, his brother and Dad, had stopped en route to collect his cousin Simon. Outside the flat where Simon lived they had found a £20 note on the floor. The fortuitous find, Lucas recalls, paid for all four of them to watch the match and to have a Wimpey dinner back at Edgware afterwards. The fact that this is vivid in his mind, and he remembers getting home and watching 'Can't Stop the Music', the Village People musical on TV, but not Arsenal's opponents that day is funny in itself.

He recalls seeing Nottingham Forest visit and Paul Hart being sent off for a horror challenge. It was the first time he had seen a red card which were far rarer back then. He also recalls the first game after Terry Neill was sacked in December 1983, for two reasons. Firstly because it was against Watford, the closest team to his home and where he would go with other family and friends on occasions. Secondly because Don Howe, in his first game, threw in a young Raphael Meade who scored a hat-trick in a 3-1 win. Lucas also looks back with some pride that Arsenal were playing several back players at that time, which he could not say about many of the teams visiting Highbury. Meade went on to score a brace in the following match which was a win at White Hart Lane.

"So my early memories of Arsenal are all with my father but by the time I was a teenager I was definitely appreciating the football more. It was when George Graham came that it all changed for Arsenal and came together for me. I think sadly in the new Arsenal area they don't talk about the George Graham era nearly enough."

YOUNG GUNNER, GEORGE GRAHAM AND DARREN DEIN

Lucas, unlike most Gunners perhaps, counts Darren Dein as a friend and it is a friendship that began at senior school. Now as a manager of footballer players such as Adebayor, Fabregas and van Persie, Darren has the unfortunate reputation of taking Arsenal's best players out of the club. *"So although we did get good money for them, he has become a bit of a fall guy but he did bring Flamini back to the club, read into that what you will! I am a fan of Flamini and outside of football he is the new Craig Johnson."*

Lucas remembers asking Darren if his dad had told him who would be taking over from Don Howe and the day it was announced, asking him all about George Graham. (He did not have a footballer sticker for Graham!) The acquaintance grew into a friendship at the same time as Graham was revitalising Arsenal on the pitch. For Dein and Lucas as for all of us, it was a wonderful time as the youngsters who had been given their head start initially by Howe, grew in stature under the new boss. Adams and Rocky were in the team, but Graham brought in Thomas, Quinn, Hayes then later Merson.

He felt the rivalry between Arsenal and Spurs at school was quite equal. Equal numbers supporting each team and the teams were quite equal at that time. We had the three FA Cup Finals at the end of the 70s and they had had the two finals in the early 80s. Spurs were, if any-thing, slightly in the ascendancy so that semi-final sequence in 1987 seemed so significant to Lucas. Those three matches for him were the making of that Graham side and the confidence and self-belief they gained that night at White Hart Lane was the start of it all.

"It was March the 4th 1987 and I was 13 on the following day. My whole birthday felt like my celebration, at school and afterwards, of Arsenal reaching their first Cup Final. It was only seven years but I would have been 6 the previous time and at that age that is about as long as you can conceive."

The final against Liverpool in the April was played the day after his Bar Mitzvah and he watched it at a family friend's house. He remem-bers that when Nicholas scored the equaliser his friend ran up and kissed Charlie on the TV and was told off by his father.

"That is when I was old enough to become a Junior Gunner. I was 13 and allowed to go without my father and with my brother and his friends. That is when it all really started for me. I was already a fan but this is when I became a home regular."

Lucas was proud to be a Junior Gunner, so proud in fact that he faked his age to keep it going for years! That of course would not be so easy today. By 1987/88 he was not missing many games at Highbury and a routine was established. The bi-weekly pilgrimage was a walk to Gunners Park then bus to Edgware. Here Lucas would meet friends and withdraw a fiver from the cashpoint; at 14 he was obviously ahead of his time. That £5 would get him his travel card for 80p and it would get

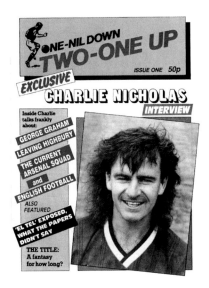

him into the game. Mostly he would pay £1.00 which later increased to £1.25 to stand in the Family Enclosure in the West Stand, and later on the North Bank, but if he felt flush he would sit for £2. Before going into the ground however, some of the remainder of the fiver would be spent with Mrs Zee for sweets at the tiny kiosk opposite the exit at Arsenal Station, by the North Bank entrance. With dessert pocketed, Lucas and friends would walk down to the Golden Fish Bar in Gillespie Road to get some chips for their first course. Occasionally he would buy an official match day programme but even then the alternative view and the humour of the early fanzines would appeal more.

"I would sometimes buy a programme but often buy the Arsenal Echo Echo and 1 Nil Down 2 One up. I feel like the Echo was very cheap and the first fanzine."

When asked if the classic George Dawes 'Peanuts' song from Shooting Stars was inspired by the Highbury peanut sellers the answer was yes. Was there enough left from the fiver after tube, sweets, chips, fanzine and entrance to invest in what was essentially bird food?

"Yes absolutely, the Percy Daltons' peanuts, 40p a bag. You know what I used to do? I used to buy those peanuts every week. I used to think I must go and get those peanuts, very important. Spend the match cracking the shells and most would fall to the floor and you would eat them still in that horrible skin. I would get to the end of the bag and think to myself I don't really like these peanuts. Next week I would hear the cry 'Peanuts' and off I would go and buy them again."

Towards the end of his first season as a regular Lucas managed to get a ticket for the League Cup Final but in a way wished he hadn't. His first final at Wembley was to end not only with a devastating defeat as he watched on from behind the goal where Nigel Winterburn missed his penalty, but also the day was made worse by the fact that he got poked in the eye during the second Arsenal goal celebration with the flag stick of the flag he had bought outside the ground.

1988–1992

By the season Arsenal were to win the title historically at Anfield, Lucas was only missing the occasional school night match on the insistence of his mum. He felt he must have been to about 20 games that season and at 14 was obsessed. *"It was such a passion and I was by then totally fanatical."*

Of course at 14 you are not worldly wise and Lucas recalls the day of Hillsborough with some slight embarrassment. He had applied to be a ball boy through his Junior Gunner membership and had been successful. The match he has been allocated was the visit of Newcastle on the 15th April, on the same day Liverpool and Nottingham Forest were to battle it out in their FA Cup Semi-Final at Hillsborough. Lost in the excitement of the occasion Lucas had come into the Player's Lounge at half time and glibly asked what the Tottenham score was.

Everyone was watching the tragic events unfold on the television. *"Everyone looked at me oddly but I was only 14 and had not truly realised the severity of what was happening and how serious it was."* In hindsight and based on his own childhood experiences on the terraces at Highbury and on seeing the fences at Wembley at his first ever match, Lucas is extremely proud that his club never erected fences. Hillsborough was the accident waiting to happen but it would not have happened at Highbury.

On the evening that the league was to be decided, Friday 26th May 1989, he and his brother, with another friend of his brother's and his brother, 4 Gooners, headed to a friend's house. The friend was a Liverpool fan so when the final whistle went and the improbable had occurred, staying there was not an option of course. The four ecstatic friends headed straight for Highbury in his brother's car, to join fellow fans celebrating Arsenal's first title in 18 years.

"We had a cassette single in the car with 'Good Old Arsenal' on and we had it blaring out full volume with the windows down. When

we got there we parked up and were just running around outside the Marble Halls. Fans were just randomly running up and kissing the Marble Halls, It was just glorious!"

He still has a photo, proudly displayed on the wall in his bathroom, of his brother and himself with George Graham and Bobby Moore at a signing, at Brent Cross Shopping Centre when they released the single 'Back Where We Belong'. He bought a 12-inch version, which he still has, and on the same day the VHS of the season's highlights was released.

1987 to 1992 represented a fabulous time for Arsenal and one of Lucas's favourite periods as a Gunner. The second title in 3 seasons in 1990/91 was majestic. He was still going to every home game but in 1992 came one of the saddest moments he had experienced as a supporter, the decision by Graham to sell Rocky. This on the back of selling Michael Thomas was a pivotal moment and Graham's ruthless streak marked a turning point for Lucas. 91/92 was to be his last season as a regular for a while.

THE CHELSEA AND BRISTOL WILDERNESS YEARS

In summer before the 1992 season, still reeling from the Rocky sale and waiting on his A Level results, Lucas had made an important decision that was to shape his life to a degree. That decision was, that rather than go straight to university, he wanted to take a gap year and try and do stand-up comedy. Thankfully for all of us Mrs Lucas backed her son's decision with one provison, which was that he had to make a financial contribution to the household. Lucas was not anticipating making much from his alternative brand of stand up straight away, although as it transpired he did, so some gainful employment was required.

During his sixth form Lucas had been helping run some youth groups at his local synagogue and there were a couple of kids he would babysit for. Their father was a man called Clive Pollard. It's where he got the name for his Bristol chav creation Vicky Pollard. Clive had lots of different business interests importing various sports merchandise. If you recall the mini football kits you used to stick in car windows, the man behind that craze was Clive Pollard. He was a big Chelsea fan and got the franchise to run the CFC club shop. So to make the weekly contribution his mother had asked for, Lucas found himself working at Chelsea football club shop by day and performing at night.

So for the first time since the early in a decade he found himself not being a regular at Highbury whilst ironically being a regular for very different reasons at Stamford Bridge. Oddly none of the staff, barring the Saturday boy, were Chelsea fans, with the manager being Watford and the other regular member of staff a Leeds fan. The three of them would endlessly tease Kenny the young part-timer as Chelsea were so poor back then.

"I obviously had no affinity with Chelsea but I had to wear the away shirt as part of my uniform so I would often wear my Arsenal shirt under it."

He was able on match days, to watch the action from the Shed for about 30 minutes in each half and saw Arsenal in action there twice. Obviously he was not foolhardy enough to cheer for the Arsenal so he swiftly decided the next best thing which was to berate Chelsea. One particularly fine display by Arsenal saw a 2-0 win that recalls.

"No one berates a team more than their own fans, so I spent the match just shouting 'Chelsea you're fucking shit!' every time they did something wrong and sarcastically applauding the Arsenal goals. That was a source of pleasure."

In the autumn of 1993 Lucas went to Bristol following in the footsteps of his friend David Walliams who whilst older, he had met at the National Youth Theatre in school holidays. His time in Bristol was spent studying and at lectures during the week and doing stand-up at the weekends. His relationship with Arsenal changed because of his lifestyle and the distance but it was not only that. Money was tight and with the advent of the Premier League and the cost of stadium improvements required in the wake of the Taylor Report, prices for football had jumped considerably. The quality and brand of football at that time was also a factor.

"If I am honest the later Graham Arsenal had become quite dull to watch. As much as you're a fan, you can love the club but you don't always love the team. In fact sometimes you don't love the team because you love the club. You just feel like 'what is going on?'"

By 1995 the comedy had taken off so much that Lucas dropped out after only two years of his university course. By then he had appeared on Vic Reeves and Bob Mortimer's show "The Smell of Reeves and Mortimer" and in the September his new character, George Dawes hit our screens in Shooting Stars and he would not look back. Back in London and less the impoverisheed student, his relationship with Arsenal was to change and his dormant love to be re-kindled.

"I guess like everyone I was revitalised when that strange foreign chap with the big glasses came in 1996. When Wenger came I started going to Highbury again when my work schedule allowed it."

DELICIOUS 1998 AND 2002

Back in the fold but no longer a Junior Gunner, Lucas quite often relied on friends to get him tickets at Highbury. One such occasion was the final game of the 1998 Premier League campaign. He had met Lee Dixon when he had been at a Pet Shop Boys gig with David Walliams at the Savoy the previous summer. Dixon was a pal of Chris Lowe from the band, a massive Gooner, and he has introduced the two of them. Dixon and Lucas stayed in touch and have been friends ever since.

"Lee got me one ticket for the 4-0 Everton game. It was behind a pillar but I was there and the pillar only blocked my view of the middle of the pitch. It did not matter and I still saw all the goals including the majestic Adams finale."

Having seen the league won in such style, he had been desperate to get a ticket for the FA Cup Final and to hopefully see Arsenal secure an historic double. At the time of course it was pre Little Britain and he was only known for George Dawes and his network was not extensive. He was doing some writing on a TV show for Keith Allen called "You Are Here" and Allen managed to get hold of two tickets on the Friday night before the Wembley showcase.

The condition was that Lucas took Keith's son, Alfie (now in Game of Thrones, then aged ten), to the match. Lucas took Alfie and also went with his friend Paul Kaye who had recently retired his first comic creation Dennis Penis. More of Kaye in the next chapter, but Lucas went to many a game with Kaye and describes him as the *'biggest Arsenal fan I know.'*

Lucas also suffered the disappointment of the Liverpool defeat in 2001 in Cardiff, that time with his brother and Kaye. The same trio returned to Cardiff the following season to see the glorious win over Chelsea to secure Wenger's second League and FA Cup Double. For Lucas the 2001/2 campaign was the perfect Arsenal season, surpassing the 2003/4 unbeaten Premier League season.

"That felt like the absolute peak to me and so special because Pires had been so imperious that season and then got injured and then Freddie just stepped up so magnificently moved to the left and just became Pires."

Matt Lucas hosting the 2013 AFC Foundation Ball

LUCAS AND ARSENAL TODAY

For a while, when Little Britain was simply the biggest show on television, Lucas took a box at the Emirates as mentioned earlier. Of course it was a way to guarantee being able to go to every game and invite friends and to contribute to the club. He has been proud to be an ambassador for the 'Gay Gooners' and to host events, such as two AFC Foundation Balls, for them.

He has lived in America for the most part of the last five years so, once again as in 1992 his relationship with Arsenal Football Club has changed. He will still get up early if needs be to watch a match or record and get up early and watch as if live, but sadly he feels the Emirates has not quite yet had the football it deserves.

If things are not quite perfect on the pitch he is hugely proud of modern Arsenal in other ways and in particular, given his own sexuality, their stance on homosexuality.

"I can never have conceived growing up that there would be an official Arsenal Gay, LGBT Supporters group and that the club would be so welcoming to all different types of people and see that as a worthwhile endeavour. I would never have imagined it happening in the 1980s and

photo courtesy of Stuart Macfarlane and Arsenal FC

not every club does it. Some might say what has that got to do with football but it was not just the anti-Semitic stuff and hearing the Auschwitz chant which offended me as a Jew that I had to listen to growing up on the terraces there was a lot of homophobia."

In truth Lucas, unlike perhaps some, does not readily accept the view that the influx of money has changed the game for the worse. He accepts that there are great aspects that have been lost through the changes in the game; Bosman, Hillsborough, Taylor and Sky have all contributed to making football became more middle class and become the domain of the broadsheets as much as the tabloids.

"But I think also there are things that we have gained. Like being able to go to the toilet in a ground and actually have toilet paper and a sink to wash your hands. I like the fact that people generally behave better particularly having been frightened for my life in the mid to late eighties in the crushes. I did not feel truly safe at Highbury then and I now feel far safer and more protected at football."

Lucas has no wish to comment on the present Arsenal, other than to say that football does go in cycles and there are peaks and troughs. There always have been and there always will be. He is very conscious that fans of other clubs must laugh at our infighting and constant moaning and see us as feeling somehow 'entitled' as Arsenal fans. We can close the chapter with some sound wisdom from Matt Lucas and a check on the scores with George Dawes:

'I love Arsenal and I know that we are not in the happiest spell at the moment. Sometimes football clubs make it hard to love them but I still love them. I am just glad there's soft toilet paper when you go to the toilet now.'"

What are the scores, George Dawes?

Arsenal 4 Everton 0!

PAUL KAYE, THE TWO GREAT ARSENAL DENNISES OF '95

1995 saw the arrival of arguably Arsenal's greatest ever player, Dennis Bergkamp. It also saw Paul Kaye's comic alter ego Dennis Pennis explode onto our screens on the BBC. With bright red hair, thick framed glasses, a squeaky voice and more brazen front than many felt comfortable with, Pennis and his camera crew waited outside film premieres or anywhere the character might catch unsuspecting celebrities unawares. His questions varied from rude to insulting and left the celebrities, frequently American, bemused or angry and the viewing audience in tears. The excruciatingly painful yet hilarious results were weaved together with other pre-filmed Pennis sketches and caught the imagination of the youth of the nation for two short years. Pennis, like his creator Kaye, was a Gooner and when dressed down was seen in a 1970s yellow away kit and when dressed up for premieres always sported an Arsenal lapel badge and often a scarf.

Kaye's Dennis was ahead of his time and he arguably inspired many others such as Sacha Baron Cohen to follow his daring lead. Kaye sometimes regrets effectively killing off his creation after only 3 half hour shows, but for a character that existed for such a short space of time he is fondly remembered by millions and to an extent still defines Kaye. In the close to 20 years since Pennis bid farewell, Kaye has created another alter-ego in brash, foul-mouthed American Mike Strutter on MTV, and appeared in numerous comedy shows and films both sides on the Atlantic. Kaye more recently won acclaim on the West End

The demise of Pennis in 1997 – note the tie pin!

stage and of course in a small TV show called Game of Thrones. Even with all his success, to many, he will always be Dennis Pennis first and foremost and Kaye sort of knew that would be the case.

"I made life quite tricky for myself because once you have outed yourself as a character like that it is hard to live it down. Even now, so many years later, I hear Dennis Pennis is at the National Theatre or Dennis Pennis is back in Game of Thrones. It's just the way it is. I loved my idea of Pennis more than actually doing it, but once I had finished doing it I knew for me that was it and that I didn't want to do anything like it again. I didn't know what else to do with the character and thought it had run its course, but in hindsight there was so much more I could have done with it. I was offered a chat show but I thought that would be the antithesis of what the character was all about. Taking the piss out of people who were being paid three grand to sit there felt a bit whiffy to me."

However successful Kaye has been, before he was a comedian and then an actor, he was and is first and foremost a Gooner, an artist and a punk. The Arsenal loyalty is sneaked into his work where possible; most blatantly in the award winning 2005 Mockumentary film 'It's All Gone Pete Tong' in which Kaye's main character, deaf DJ, Frankie Wilde, sported the yellow and blue chevron 1992 away shirt. He surreptitiously slipped his Arsenal love into an early employment at White Hart Lane and the truth behind that legend later. First though, let us start at the beginning of a thoroughly enjoyable and entertaining romp through near on half a century of Kaye's journey with his beloved Gunners.

FROM THE BEGINNING

For Kaye, the Arsenal support came straight from his 'old man'. Aged seven, he confesses to not remembering the 1971 FA Cup Final but vividly recalls looking at the back of the Sunday Express and seeing the picture of Charlie George flat out in celebration. George was his first hero and the player to identify with, *"He had everything about him I loved. Class, swagger and of course he was one of us, a North Bank boy."*

His family lived in Wembley, a fact he was always proud of as it gave him an identity on his summer holidays to Spain. The following year when Arsenal again reached the final, but lost to Leeds, he recalls being in Wembley High Road after the match. There was a coach of

Kaye at his beloved Highbury

Leeds supporters so Kaye and his mate 'flicked the v's at them'. The angry Leeds fans began aggressively banging on the coach windows and the two boys, suddenly feeling less brave, ran all the way home to Kaye's house and hid in the cupboard under the stairs for two hours.

His dad took him to his first game at Highbury in September 1973 when he was eight-years-old. It was against Stoke and the Gunners obligingly won 2-1 with goals from Ball and Radford. It had been a surprise for young Kaye when his dad told him on leaving the synagogue that he was taking him somewhere very special for a treat. He had not had a clue where he was being taken but they duly arrived at the temple of Highbury and took their seats in the East Stand. The match was enjoyable but something else grabbed Kaye's attention.

"I could not take my eyes off the North Bank. This steaming mass of people, swaying and singing and I thought 'fucking wow,' I want to be in there!"

The North Bank was to come soon after with his older cousin Richard who was a mentor and role model for Kaye. Four years older, it was Richard that he aspired to be like and who got him into smoking, punk and crucially the North Bank. So in the mid-70s he would go with Richard and stand in the middle of the great terrace he had admired on his first visit; still too small and only able to see half of the action but just thriving on the atmosphere. As befitting a young punk, pogoing to see his heroes seemed perfect.

"I used to just love the North Bank. I had a 'North Bank Rules' badge the size of a saucer which I was very proud of. The first real punks I saw were in there. One guy I remember so well with bright blue hair and a donkey jacket with 'The Clash' painted on the back of it. So many characters in there it was so exciting to feel a part of it. There were so many songs back then. Plus you could swear your head off very loudly! For an eleven-year-old that was very liberating and it felt genuinely dangerous. Those were great years; Sammy Nelson mooning at us, George Armstrong scoring direct from a corner against Man United and Super Mac's hat trick in a 5-3 classic against Newcastle. Best of all though was getting my first FA Cup semi-final ticket for the Arsenal v Orient game in 1978 after queuing round Highbury all day with my programme vouchers. That was the happiest day of my young life."

Of course the most famous punk at that time was an Arsenal fan.

"One of the great things about being a punk was that John Lydon was a Gooner. I have never met him although I would love to. I remember getting a pull-out poster from the Record Mirror. I was examining all the badges he was wearing and there it was a fucking Arsenal badge! I was like of course! Who else could someone that cool support?"

Touching on the fierce anti-Semitic chanting that was evident at that time this must have impacted him as a Jewish Gooner?

"I remember it at Arsenal v Spurs games and I particularly remember the hissing. I don't remember ever feeling threatened by it but, yes, completely appalled. Something comes over people at football, often the humour is incredible but there is also the pure fucking ignorance out there."

As a punk at that time there was a certain uncomfortable irony that his hero, Sid Vicious, had purportedly written the lyrics to 'Belsen is a Gas' by the Sex Pistols, *"That didn't bother me so much because it just felt really naughty, but I had a mate who would make his excuses and go to the toilet when we were all pogoing to that song and in retrospect I wish I'd done the same."*

Strange too, that the only time he has been ejected, although only by association, was for mild homophobic chanting when the anti-Semitic songs were accepted back then. It was at home to Red Star Belgrade in December 1978 just after the tabloids had outed then Liberal leader, Jeremy Thorpe, a married man, for an affair with Norman Scott. Kaye recalls his older cousin Rich and his mate Nick had attempted to start up a chant in the North Bank to the tune of 'Knees up Mother Brown', along the lines of, "'Knees up Jeremy Thorpe, knees up Jeremy Thorpe. Norman, Norman, Norman, Norman, Norman, Norman Scott!". Homophobia was hardly a terrace issue back then and the song was intended in jest, not to incite, but the two older lads were hauled out by the cops by their scarves. Kaye and his younger cousin Pete had to follow them out so as not to be left on their own in the North Bank. Perhaps not their finest hour but Nick and Richard will return as heroes later in the Kaye Arsenal memoirs.

PRE-MATCH RITUALS AND MISSING THE HIGHBURY OF THE LATE 1980S AND 90S

Kaye is unashamedly nostalgic about the Arsenal match day experience and the Highbury of his youth. He loved the impromptu nature of it all back then. Meeting at the Sir George Robey pub in Finsbury Park, not knowing if there would be five of you or twenty and then, after a few pints, paying on the door and being packed into the North Bank like sardines.

It is not just the sterile atmosphere inside the ground today but the build-up, singing and buzz that grew outside the ground beforehand. Today, as he approaches the Emirates, he bemoans the lack of pre-match chanting at the ground. He and friends affectionately take the mick out of fellow fans as they walk under the railway bridge on Hornsey Road. As it has an echo in the tunnel, it's literally the only place that any singing can be heard on that route to the stadium. "You only sing in the tunnel!" is the chant.

HATS SCARVES AND BADGES

As we have established, Kaye loved the whole build-up and as with many fans this entails routines and rituals. Some are set in stone and some come and go, like Nick Hornby with his sugar mice in 'Fever Pitch'. He recalls how one such ritual was established one night before playing a German team in a European fixture. At the top of St Thomas' Road there was this old chap who used to sell hats, scarves and badges, "Get your hats, scarves and badges here!"

"We were playing a German side in the UEFA Cup I think and we decided to ask him for a badge he obviously would not have. So we enquired as to whether he had a badge with 'Fuck the Germans' written on it? He looked on his board and there it was a badge with 'Fuck the Germans' on it"!

The Pint on the Wall Gang 2002

The badge was proffered and even though it was exactly what Kaye and his mates had asked for they declined to purchase. So from that point on they would go to him every game and he never seemed to let on that he knew them or remembered their antics. Each home game for months they would arrive at his stall and proceed to scan the board for the most ridiculous or obscure badge he had on his board before asking for it.

"'Mate, you haven't got a badge with 'My Mum is a Jacket Potato' on it have you, yellow lettering on mauve background?' He would find it, say 'there you go' and we would look at it for a while and then say 'you know what, mate, I think we're going to leave it'."

PINT ON THE WALL GANG

In the 90s, having moved from the George Robey to the Auld Triangle the pre-match ritualists had become a gang called the 'Pint on the Wall Gang'. Why, because there was a wall there, opposite the pub, and they would have a pint on it! Another member, briefly of the Pint on the Wall Gang, was Poppy Teacher who of course is now Tony Adams' wife. Kaye had met her when she worked as a researcher for Johnny Vaughn's Production Company.

"I met her on a job and she was so lovely. We hooked up before a few games and she became part of the gang. She came for a while

and then disappeared, and the next time I saw her she was on the top of the Arsenal victory parade bus with Tony when we had won the 'Double' in 2002."

NIGEL WINTERBURN

Of course the pre-match singing of the player's names, as they warmed up in the ground, has disappeared with advanced ticket purchase and this, for Kaye, is another nail in the coffin containing pre-match atmosphere. Back in 1988 though it was still very much part of the North Bank's warm up and Kaye and his mates felt a special bond with Nigel Winterburn. On his home debut Kaye and his companions were positioned to the lower left of the terrace. Just before kick-off they all shouted out as one "NIGEL!" at the tops of their collective voices, to which the delighted debutant feeling welcome had turned and given them a thumbs up. Kaye and his crew, delighted at the bond with the new Gooner, cheered back. A new ritual was born and from then on literally every home game he played they would all shout out "NIGEL!" and he would turn round and give them the thumbs up.

"Then, after years of this, we happened to wangle our way into the player's bar after a game and when Nigel came in we all rushed at him. We were all talking at once saying, 'You know just before kick-off every home game for the last 10 years there's a bunch of guys who shout Nigel and you always give them the thumbs up? Well, that's us!' He just sort of looked at us as if we were deranged, turned round and walked off. We had all expected him to go, 'Oh my God it was you guys', but in reality he didn't give a shit!"

They do say never meet your heroes, but luckily for Kaye 'Nutty Nigel' was the exception to the rule and he has been blessed in interacting with many Arsenal legends; but not before he was to interact with a few Spurs players. No, this is not a joke and nor is it a myth.

BEHIND ENEMY LINES

Paul Kaye's first real job post university was unbelievably at White Hart Lane as a designer. Much has been written or said about what he did or did not do to sabotage Spurs material as a Gooner behind enemy lines, so what is the truth of it?

"I got the job in 1989 and was there until 1991, so I was there when we won the league in '89 so perfect timing. I would go in every day

with my Arsenal hat on and there would be David Howells and Steve Sedgely saying, 'Get that fucking hat off!'. It was beautiful winding them all up."

The nicest chap there was Gazza, who was still relatively sane at the point as Kaye reflects. He was not so complimentary about the then boss Terry Venables, who was there "with enormous sweat patches under the arms of his lilac shirt at 9.30 in the morning".

At that time off the pitch, and obviously not on it, Spurs in a marketing sense were well ahead of their time and Kaye was not only doing designs for their merchandise but all other teams using Hummel kits.

"I had a little office at White Hart Lane and could see the cockerel clock out of my window. It was the first job I got where I was earning some proper money but what a fucking whore I was. Talk about working behind enemy lines."

The Arsenal sabotage came in the form of a small Arsenal cannon – pointing the right way – on the front of the autumn catalogue, hidden in a pen and ink drawing of the new stand. A closer inspection would have revealed hundreds of small faces and his hidden Gunner image. So the myth is not a myth but the truth, although perhaps not as extreme as word of mouth may have led some to believe over the years.

"The story had been exaggerated over time to the point where I get told I had designed a huge cockerel image made up of thousands of little cannons, so you are absolutely welcome to make anything up and embellish at will."

Whilst he feels he should have hated working at The Lane the job was enjoyable, doing caricatures of the players for pencil cases and lunch boxes whilst constantly talking mick out of them with his Arsenal hat on. With Arsenal having won the league in such spectacular fashion at Anfield it was a joy to be there and it was also fascinating to see the inner workings of a football club, even that one. Thankfully he had left again with perfect timing, before the 1991 FA Cup semi-final. Indeed the only scar left on Kaye from his time as a double agent was an impression of Ray Clemence that he cannot shake.

"I have got this thing about Ray Clemence who I'd actually loved when I was a kid mostly because of his yellow admiral kit. I'm a kit nut and don't Puma make shit ones by the way? I used to walk past Ray's office a lot because it was on the way to the photocopier. Every time I walked past his door he'd just be sat behind his desk staring at a bottle of Tippex. Never ever saw him do anything and it has given me an opinion about him. He would turn up on the bench at England games and I

would be shouting 'shit' at him on the tele and people would say, 'Paul, what is your problem with Ray Clemence?' I'm over it now."

Kaye left his role at Spurs to play in punk bands, work in pubs, design theatre posters and to travel to and work in Israel. Pennis was to arrive on our screens four years later in 1995 but his first true Arsenal claim to fame came much earlier and shortly after exiting White Hart Lane.

GEORGE KNOWS

In the 1990/91 season it was the day after it was announced Arsenal were to be deducted two points for the brawl at Old Trafford. Kaye put his whole dole cheque on Arsenal winning the league. He has never made a bet before or since, which he describes as a blessing as he would not even have a roof over his head if that addiction had taken hold of him. The simple chant of "stick the two points up your arse" on the night we won the league in '91 was for Paul the greatest chant he ever had the pleasure to bellow out in the North Bank.

As it transpired the Arsenal management and team as a collective had proverbially stuck the two points where the sun did not proverbially shine, and by early May were closing in on a second league title in three years. In the first week of May, Kaye took a call from his cousin Richard, who by then was a West Upper man with some of his mates, who needed a favour.

Richard and his friends had picked up a catchphrase from ex-Arsenal boss Terry Neill, then co-commentator on Capital Gold. That phrase, delivered in Neill's Irish brogue was, 'George knows'. Whenever Jonathan Pierce would ask him a question about the Arsenal, Neill would deliver his stock answer, 'George knows'.

Having drawn away at Sunderland on May 4, Arsenal could potentially clinch the title on the 6th. Richard and his friend Nick wanted Kaye to paint them a banner for the match on his cousin's bed sheet, with the simple two words 'George knows'. Kaye had given his view, in no uncertain terms, that basically he thought it was a shocking idea because the Gunners could be crowned champions that day if they won and Liverpool failed to win at Nottingham Forest. It should be 'King George'. Despite his reservations Kaye painted the banner the night before, allowed it to dry and then delivered it to Nick and Richard at the George Robey. They were all meeting there to watch the Liverpool match. He again told them he thought they had fucked up with their weak Neill inspired slogan.

Of course Kaye was ultimately proved wrong. Liverpool did lose, Arsenal did win, the team were crowned champions and photos of the 'George Knows' banner, hanging over the front of the West Upper, by Nick and Richard were all over the papers the next morning and mentioned in many match reports.

However, for Kaye, Richard, Nick and their friends it was to get so much better. In 1993 when Kaye was in Tel Aviv he was reading and loving, as all Gunners have, Nick Hornby's Fever Pitch.

"Of course I got to the end of the chapter, I think it was page 171 and there it was; Hornby wrote, 'And there was a banner flying in the West Upper that night that said simply 'George knows' and George did know like fathers rarely do.' I have never had goose bumps like that in my life! It was such a buzz to have that preserved in probably the most important football book ever written, well certainly for us."

Kaye was to meet Hornby years later at a radio station and he told him that it was him who had painted the banner. He is not sure the author believed him but he still felt a massive personal connection.

"It was such a magical feeling to read that book and feel like I had a part to play in the story, special beyond words, but had it been down to me it would have said 'King George' and it may not have been in the book because there were quite a few King banners that day. Of course we also unknowingly started something because we now have Arsene Knows!"

He laughs now, not just because he painted something that became part of Highbury folklore in more ways than one and he is proud of it, but also at the irony as he so vividly recalls handing the banner to Nick in the pub and saying, "Trust me, this is a really shit idea mate."

MEETING YOUR HEROES – DAVID SEAMAN

This anecdote began with Kaye saying, "Matt [Lucas] must have told you about when we rang David Seaman while drunk at three o'clock in the morning after we won the Double in 1998?" Having established that indeed Matt had, Kaye decided to take me back to when he met the Arsenal keeper to set the scene.

He had met David at the Comedy Awards in 1997. Kaye had been nominated for his first ever award, Best Newcomer, for Dennis Pennis. He recollects being extremely nervous, undoubtedly drinking too much and thinking that whoever comes out with the nominations and to present the award it would be a sign as to whether he had won or not. *"Then out came David Seaman with the nominations and I was sat there thinking 'I've fucking won it!' Never trust a lucky omen...it went to the guy from the Thin Blue Line."*

Not wishing to miss the opportunity, Kaye caught up with the Arsenal legend at the after show party, as he was keen to tell him that, unbeknownst to Seaman, he has had a very lucky escape from Pennis himself the previous year. Kaye had heard Seaman was due at an event and it was around the time that there had been too many stories about footballers misbehaving, David's team mate Ray Parlour for one. Consequently, he had mocked up a back page of The Sun with a lurid headline, which they were going to thrust in front of the keeper asking if he had seen it and would care to comment.

'Wenger fires Seaman over Bender!' was the fabulously funny headline but unfortunately Seaman had not come to the event and the classic idea for a Pennis gag had remained an idea. Kaye and Seaman bonded over the story and swapped numbers.

Fast forward to May 1998. Kaye and six or seven others, including Matt Lucas and Alfie Allen, as we have learned, were at Wembley to see Wenger's first League and Cup Double secured. Having dropped Alfie off, the grown-ups proceeded to Soho to behave unlike grown-ups. Or in Kaye's words,

"We got fucking wankered! We were looking for Newcastle fans in Soho and we hadn't found any at all! So we gave up and went to a club called GG's, which was an arty sort of place in a basement on Wardour Street, and by this point we were pretty out of control. We all walked into this basement, pissed up and celebrating but disappointed we'd not found any Geordies and the first two people we see down there are Ant and Dec (huge laughter). They lasted about thirty seconds and ran out. I have never met then before or since. Spent all night looking for Geordies, find none and then all of a sudden find the two most famous ones there's ever been. It was a joyous and beautiful thing...but not for them."

Three days later Lucas and Kaye were again together, filming a show in Leeds and again out on the town in the evening very drunk. For some reason, back at their hotel, Kaye recalled having Seaman's mobile number on his phone and the two friends decided they should call him to personally congratulate him on winning the Double. Having told him how special he was "we just sang Arsenal sings down the phone to him for about an hour. It was fantastic, very funny and he was amazingly good natured about it."

Kaye shares a joke with Lee Dixon

THANKS TO YOUR HEROES... LEE DIXON

After the launch of the club's debenture scheme and the advent of the Premier League, Kaye had found himself priced out of regular attendance. Of course the success of Pennis changed things financially; however, during the mid-90s he was often as likely to watch the matches in pubs as in the ground. He vividly remembers watching the 1995 Cup Winners Cup Final defeat in the pub, but not only because of Nayim's late winner.

"One of the funniest things I have ever seen was the night we lost to Real Zaragoza. I was in the Highbury Barn and at the end of an awful night the cameraman was just lingering on the hero for them, Nayim, a hideous man. All of a sudden some bloke just jumped up on a table and glassed the telly. It was kind of worth being there just for that because it is not the type of thing you are ever likely to see again and it got the biggest cheer of the night."

A few years later Kaye was to get his first season ticket with a little help from a certain Lee Dixon. Kaye had been asked to write a piece for the Arsenal right-back legend's testimonial brochure, which he was delighted to do. This was in 1997 and Dixon had called him to thank him, so Kaye decided if you don't ask you don't get and asked if Lee would by any chance wrangle a season ticket or two? Kaye ended up going down to meet Lee Dixon at the ground and the player ended up sourcing three season tickets. He thinks they were something to do with UEFA but Dixon "put us in touch with a man who could!"

Kaye still has the three seats today, which he and close friend Jon Glazer, director of Sexy Beast fame, and their mate Pete (his cousin Rich's younger brother!) share with their sons.

Nice one, Lee!

MEETING YOUR HEROES... IAN WRIGHT

Kaye has been fortunate enough to meet Ian Wright a few times. He was doing some filming and then some Mike Strutter gigs in London and Wrighty turned up to one at the Angel.

"He was in my dressing room after the gig and we were just singing Arsenal songs. I woke up the next morning and thought I'd dreamt it."

That was in October 2008 and a week or so later he was at home on the day that Obama was elected President of the United States of America, November 4th.

"Just when I thought the day could not get better the postman arrived with a delivery for me. It was a framed picture from Ian Wright. 'Dear Paul, I love you, Ian Wright' written on a photo of him celebrating, having just broken the goal scoring record. I have met him a couple of times since and he's everything you want him to be, funny, always charming and a proper Gooner."

WRITING FOR 'THE ARSENAL MAGAZINE' 2002 – 2008

Kaye tells me that back in the day he would occasionally go to the Plimsoll afterwards, where all the original Clock End Boys were, and try and get songs off the ground. No matter how hard he tried nothing they came up with seemed to take off.

"We would get tanked up and go in there where all the boys were and there was a sort of raised area. To my mind we came up with the best song ever that never caught on about Sylvain Wiltord. It was to the Carly Simon hit 'You're So Vain, 'You're Sylvain, I bet you think this song is about you. You're Sylvain, I bet you think this song is about you, don't you? Don't you?' I have been praying since 2004 that we sign another player called Sylvain because I am convinced the song is a classic."

Thankfully for Kaye someone did want him to pen a few lines and tap into his creative prose and that someone was in fact Arsenal FC. Kaye was asked to write a column for the Arsenal Magazine and he was honoured to accept and he wrote the celebrity fans feature for six years; the last two seasons at Highbury and the first four at the Emirates. Latterly, for obvious reasons to anyone reading this book, he found it mentally exhausting because he felt he had to be relentlessly positive.

"It was fun, a real privilege and wonderful to have that connection with the club but by the end though I had wrung every last upbeat anecdote out of myself. I'm a glass half-empty kind of guy, so having to turn out something so relentlessly positive over a season was really difficult! I sort of made myself believe at the start of the season, like we all do, kept it going with endlessly optimistic articles, and by the time of our usual end of season implosion I was in pieces. They were really tough times, missing Highbury like mad, the likes of Gallas and Bendtner not fit to wear the shirt – how did Gallas get the number 10? – not to mention trying to come to terms with the fact that the club had rebranded itself with our famous cannon shooting backwards! Sacrilege."

Kaye also found himself objecting to some of the modern aspects of the game and he wanted to comment or voice his objection but wasn't allowed to by the powers that be. He had a great boss, Andy Exley, who he let him away with as much as he could. Even his subtle monthly statement against his beloved Arsenal's stadium being named after an airline was censored. As Kaye said, by way of example, "In 10 years' time it could be the Twix Stadium." So, he would submit his column calling the stadium Ashburton Grove and by the time the magazine was printed the club had always changed it to the Emirates.

Kaye wants his club, a club with a fine tradition, to have a stadium with a name and a legacy but modern football is driven by money not tradition. Kaye mentions as an example from his time at the magazine when the first four rows of seats at Highbury would get taken out to allow for bigger advertising.

"I mean, you would have expected anyone who suggested that in a meeting to have been thrown out of a window. But, no, it was heard and the idea became reality. When something like that is allowed to happen and when people with tickets can't go because the adverts are more important, you know it is the beginning of the end of something, at least for my generation."

Kaye bringing some style to a photoshoot at his beloved Highbury

With the magazine role came a few perks and privileges, one such perk was being invited to host a Q&A at the Emirates on the occasion of the 50th edition of the magazine. The panel included Kenny Sansom, Charlie George and Thierry Henry, who Kaye was sitting next to and instantly clicked with.

Henry had his hand on my knee boys!

"He had his hand on my knee at one point and he just left it there while he was talking. I was trying to text my mates with my left hand (not easy) while it was still on there, 'Thierry's got his hand on my fucking knee right now!' He was saying to me, 'So, Paul, what is your favourite Arsenal kit of all time?' We bonded over the gold kit and to be honest he was just lovely, I did not sleep for about two nights afterwards. I have to look at the picture, which has pride of place in my house just to remind myself that it did actually happen."

There was also the opportunity to get in the Highbury team bath and 'pose' with the FA Cup!

"I got permission to film some Dennis Pennis DVD extras at High-bury in the spring of 2004. I got in the famous big bath with Matt Lucas (in nappies I seem to remember) and we filmed a really silly sketch in there. We'd won the FA Cup the previous year and they brought it down for us which was an unexpected treat. Unbeknownst to the High-bury staff, whilst we were alone with it, I managed to quickly strip off naked and pose holding the FA Cup over my privates. I left what can only be described as a 'cock smudge' on it and a couple of months later I thoroughly enjoyed watching Roy Keene kissing it at Wembley!"

MEETING YOUR ULTIMATE HERO... TONY ADAMS

Meeting and chatting with Paul Kaye is, for me, meeting a hero. With Pennis he created a mould and then broke it; in *Perfect World* he was David Brent years before David Brent and along with millions he transported me to another life in *Two Thousand Acres of Skye*. Our conversation about his love of Arsenal has roamed randomly through the decades but where to conclude this anecdotal romp?

There could be no other place than when Kaye met his ultimate hero. Kaye was performing as Mr Wormwood in a matinee perfor- mance of *Matilda* the Musical in the West End in 2011. When the lights went up for the curtain call and cast bow, there in the front row was Tony Adams with Poppy and their children. Kaye is an alcoholic, seven years sober, and reading Adam's book *Addicted* was one of the things that made it dawn on him that he might have a similar problem. Having seen Adams in the audience, he rushed to ask the company manger to invite Tony and his family to the stage door.

Kaye was able to give the Adams family a tour of the stage and set and witness first hand the absolute charm of the man, who had ardent Millwall and West Ham members of the stage crew coming over to shake his hand.

"At the end I did not know what to do because I wanted to hug him but didn't think that was appropriate, so I went to shake his hand and I said, 'Look I read your book many years ago, it had a big effect on my life and I am now two years sober.' He sort of put his hand on my face and said, 'I am proud of you, Paul,' and gave me a hug. In that moment in time he was my captain in the dressing room of life (ha!) and I will never forget how it made me feel. They say when you sober up that things will happen beyond your wildest dreams, miraculous things. I had spent so much time watching him from the stands over the years and it was just such an honour to have him in the audience watching me, in what I consider the best thing I've ever done, and then to share that time afterwards with him."

Kaye, as we have heard, has been fortunate and blessed to have spent some quality time with some of his heroes who have had an enormous impact on his life; none more so than Adams though, for so much more than for footballing reasons. He recalls the second testimonial against Celtic, who brought 10,000 down to watch in the driving rain, describing the way he walked slowly around the Highbury pitch that night with his hands on his hips 'like an emperor.' Then, of course, we talked about that goal for which Adams' celebratory salute is now forever enshrined in bronze.

"That Everton goal in '98, will anything more poetic ever be witnessed on a football pitch? A guy who had come through so much to score a goal like that! As Martin Tyler said in the commentary leading up to that stunning strike, 'Tony Adams, WOULD YOU BELIEVE IT?'"

As Kaye concludes, when you have witnessed moments like that, you do have to be philosophical about the relative disappointment in recent years.

"All through the 1970s and 1980s, never in my wildest dreams did I expect to see football the like of which we've seen in the last couple of decades, watching players like Bergkamp and Henry in their pomp; mind blowing. We've had an incredible time. I've got a framed cover of the Times Sport section from that era with the headline 'Arsenal are the True Heirs of Cruyff's Glorious Vision'. Spurs fans always try and tell you there's not been much between us over the years and that we're full of shit. I get it in the neck from them all the time, like I've imagined it all. But I'm 51 years old right and I've seen us win six League titles, including three doubles, we've won the league at Anfield, Old Trafford and twice at their place, we've gone an entire season unbeaten, won eight FA Cups, a Cup Winners Cup and not to mention finishing above them for 20 consecutive years. What have they seen in that time? Rikki Villa's goal and a lucky Gazza free kick. Not much is it?"

No, Paul, indeed it is not.

DARA O'BRIAIN: BETWEEN THE LINES, BUT NEVER RUNNING THE CHANNELS

Dara O'Briain follows a rich heritage of hugely successful stand-up comedians to emerge from the Emerald Isle. His rich brand of observational humour brilliantly blended with, and honed by, a sharp scientific and mathematical intellect has been entertaining thousands since he graduated from University College Dublin. His Mathematics and Theoretical Science degree has not only given a unique edge to his observational stand-up, but in recent years has made him an obvious go-to choice for presenting shows such as *Stargazing* with Brian Cox, his own *Science Show* for youngsters and in 2016 to revive the old favourite *Robot Wars*.

However, 2005 was the huge breakthrough year for O'Briain. Already a massive success on the comedy circuit, on television in Ireland and as a guest on UK Panel shows, he was the biggest selling show at the Edinburgh Festival that summer. In the same year he was offered, by the BBC, the prime job of hosting *Mock the Week*. Eleven years later he is still chairing the show that combined the best of *Have I Got News for You* and *Whose Line Is It Anyway?* and it is still as popular as ever.

Would it be fair to say that O'Briain's arrival in London and career turning-point in 2005 was the catalyst for Arsenal's barren years? Is he a showbiz fan of the Gunners jumping on the Emirates bandwagon or is his relationship with the Gunners somewhat deeper-rooted than that?

photo courtesy of Stuart Macfarlane and Arsenal FC

Dara O'Briain pitch side at the Emirates

O'Briain sees his journey with Arsenal as inextricably linked with what he describes as his football education. There is a starting point for his journey and a finishing point, and like all great comedians the story makes perfect sense and comes together at the end. Unlike his peers, however, he refers to his Arsenal journey and football education as squaring the square. This is itself, unsurprisingly, a mathematical expression coined, I read, as a humorous analogy to 'squaring the circle'. It seems even football is linked to maths and science in the mind of this genius, but there is no scientific or logical reason behind the concentration of Arsenal fans in the world of comedy.

"It is a bizarre thing that there are so many Arsenal-supporting comedians. What is it in the make-up of the person, because the age at which you decide you want to become a comedian is much later than the age at which you will pick your football team? You pick a team about seven or eight and it calcifies in your head, but you don't

discover that you are going to become a comedian until much later in your life, so there is no reason why one would follow the other. It is astonishing."

FOOTBALL AND ARSENAL EDUCATION PART ONE

The calcification of Arsenal in young Dara's brain was complete in 1980, aged eight, when seven Irish players featured for the Gunners in the 1980 FA Cup Final. There were six in the starting line-up and Sammy Nelson on the bench. As a boy, despite the obvious troubles in Northern Ireland at the time, he did not differentiate between Eire and Northern Irish players. Of course three of the seven were from north of the border. Years later he bumped into David O'Leary on a train, who told him that certainly Sammy Nelson, a second-half substitute for his Irish colleague John Devine that afternoon, would not have been happy to be regarded as Irish.

That season he was first aware of Arsenal in the playground of his all Irish-speaking boys' school in South Dublin. He remembers as he and other boys would run out at break time, the more football savvy older boys would be shouting to be 'Stapo' or 'Sunderland'. To this day he is not truly aware why Alan Sunderland was a cult hero in the Dublin playground over, say, Liam Brady, other than to say: *"No, well the creative flair player is not who a boy that age wants to be. They all want to be the goal scorer."*

Frank Stapleton, of course, was an Irish international already at that time, but perhaps it was his striking partner's heroics in the previous year's Cup Final that led to the hero worship in the Dublin playground. O'Briain had to ask who these two individuals were, and once told, that was the start of the relationship with Arsenal.

With his interest sparked, perhaps inadvertently by playground peer pressure, the next logical step for the education was to seek out Stapo and Sunderland on television. Both the BBC and ITV were available in Ireland and the first match O'Briain can recall watching was the final FA Cup Semi-Final replay against Liverpool in 1980. Brian Talbot settled what had turned out to be a four-match marathon and what ensued was the long, fabulous build up to Wembley. That cemented Arsenal as his team and the 13th minute stooped header from Trevor Brooking in the final partially prepared him for the weeks, and then years, of disappointment that were to follow.

"I can vividly still see him falling towards me in the front room at

my Granny's house. I remember going out and kicking a ball angrily against a wall for about an hour after the final whistle. I also watched the Cup Winners' Cup Final later, which was equally awful."

The first full season following the progress of Arsenal, therefore, was 1980/81, and as for so many nine year-olds, that progress was charted on the 'Shoot League Ladders' chart. Many a young fan would begin in August with the very best intention of spending a Saturday evening repositioning the 22 team tags into the new league table positions. Similar to the gusto and enthusiasm we all have for 'Fantasy Football' at the outset of a new season today, for this young lad the enthusiasm for the task lasted only as long as October.

"Of course it was a horrendously irritating thing to do after a while and you gave up. But it meant that to this day, even though I gig there, I have a really deep-seated loathing of Middlesbrough, Coventry and also Birmingham, all of whom inflicted defeats on us in that, my formative season as an Arsenal fan. I could not even wish Boro well in the Europa League Final a few years ago because of a defeat they inflicted upon us early in 1980/81."

ARSENAL, MISSING THE FOOTBALL EDUCATION AND HIGHER EDUCATION

As a young boy Dara was playing a lot of football, but as a teenager he switched to Gaelic football and hurling. So although still following the Arsenal results, because he was not playing in those formative years, he feels that he lost a great part of his football education. From 14 he was playing hurling at a high level and being coached accordingly, so when peers, who stuck with football, were immersed in their tactical football education, O'Briain missed out.

"Even now I think there are phrases everyone else uses that I still don't know. I don't know where these channels are that everyone is running in for example. There are also tactical formations that I secretly think probably don't make any difference to this day."

This blissful naivety to the intricacies of formations, to an extent, still exists and is regularly illustrated, he suggests, in his poor performances at FIFA. He is always Arsenal but he stubbornly refuses to manipulate his system to suit the opposition. Boy does he sound like someone else we all know!

In many ways his perspective is still influenced by the early playground 'Stapo and Sunderland' selection process for teams.

"The best lads in the middle of the park; the tall lads, two at the back, two at the middle and two up the front, the pituitary cases as they were referred to in a Woody Allen movie. The two big lads at the back cancel out the two big lads at the front. The central spine should be the biggest lads in the class and the little lads should be spread around the sides."

Looking at Vieira and Gilberto, in front of Campbell and Adams, then later Toure, and behind Henry and Bergkamp, and then confronting Arsenal's relative lack of success since, it is hard to argue with his schoolboy logic.

After school, O'Briain's distance from a true football education continued in the academic bubble of University College Dublin. Wrapped up in studying, drinking and a huge amount of debating, which gave rise to his love of performing in front of live audiences, his close scrutiny of Arsenal lapsed. However the 1993 FA Cup Final and replay are still a vivid memory watched in the University's bar.

Perhaps it was the alcohol imbibed on each occasion, but for O'Briain, two memories from the Union Bar's big screen are inextricably interlinked: The Arsenal versus Sheffield Wednesday FA Cup Final and the showing of the original *Star Wars* series.

He recalls being one of only three students in the whole bar cheering for Arsenal, who were at that time fairly functional and unpopular. That fact was combined with the Gunners being favourites, and we all know that when there is no allegiance the tendency is for the crowd to side with the underdog. Over the three preceding Fridays, the bar had shown the initial Star Wars epics, which had proved a huge draw for the undergraduates who had not seen them since childhood. One lad, quite brilliantly as O'Briain recalls, decided for fun to side with Darth Vader from the outset, cheered every time the anti-hero appeared on the screen and when he had the apparent upper hand. Obviously the 'Vader fanboy' had a great middle Friday when the Empire struck back, and the celebrations when 'Alderaan' was obliterated by the Death Star were hilarious.

"So like a week later when they were showing the Cup Final I felt like the lad who had been cheering Vader. It felt as if that latter day George Graham's Arsenal were like Vader and were the Dark Side of the Force. So when we won the FA Cup it was like the Empire Strikes Back. In fact as soon as we had won the screen was buzzing, and rolling up as no one wanted to see the baddies lift the trophy, so the three of us storm troopers had to run and find a house to watch the boys receive the Cup."

Perhaps the only conscious addition to his football education during his time at UCD was the surprise discovery of *Fever Pitch* in the college library. He has no idea how, or why, it made the cut but obviously someone very wise had made the decision. Although bizarrely, when O'Briain had randomly typed in Arsenal that day two books had popped up. One was Hornby's seminal work, which he borrowed and devoured there and then, and the other was the *Shoot* Annual 1982, which he didn't.

FOOTBALL, A CURRENCY IN THE WORKPLACE

"So flying the Arsenal flag quietly in Ireland all changes when you begin to work and the currency of football suddenly becomes really important again."

O'Briain fell in love with debating at university and in 1994 won the *Irish Times* National Debating Championship. His calling was clearly not science at that time, and he fell in love with the buzz of standing up in front of a crowd.

"I knew I wanted to do something that involved performing in some sense. I loved the stand up and was building that but there is no instant success; you have to do other jobs while you are doing it and mine just happened to be kids' TV.

Working in children's TV is the only work you are likely to get direct from university in that medium. It is where, he explains, you can make mistakes and do your worst, where fewer people are likely to see you, whilst learning the basics, such as *'to look at the right camera and not the furniture.'*

Most of the work for RTE was in the office, with the filming of *Echo Island* representing a minimal part of his working week. It was in the office environ that immediately colleagues of different ages were talking football non-stop. He found almost from the first week that being able to talk football and hold his ground to some degree was instantly a really big deal.

"Men are unusual in the way they communicate. I think we are different anthropologically in the way we communicate – I was very happy with this, a sort of short hand, specifically for football."

So conversations about who he rated or did not rate, who was developing well and who should be bought or sold became a crucial currency and having a view was essential. Being a Gooner was tough in mid-1990s – Ireland at the height of the Man United tyranny, where the majority of his peers and virtually all the nine to fourteen year-olds on the show were United devotees. Apart from United, the only other significant swell of alternative support was for Aston Villa because of Houghton, McGrath, Staunton and Townsend. Those nine year-olds were latching on to the team with the Irish core as O'Briain had done at the same age.

"It was tough but, looking back, it was certainly handy to be affiliated with a team and it in a way became part of your identity. It was like going out and having a smoke with your boss would be today. I had no idea how important following a football team and enjoying talking about it would be. Men find it emotionally difficult to talk about things, but they find it easy to talk emotionally about football."

So, as an adult in the work place, Arsenal was back in his life, his football education was vigorously renewed and indeed became essential both with his colleagues and with his young audience. He even set up an early Fantasy League for viewers of his show, but after three or four years 'hard yards', as they say in the business, the stand-up vocation was set to overtake the day job.

FIRST MATCH AND HOLLOWAY ROAD

O'Briain did not get to a match at Arsenal until the end of the 2002/03 season, by which time his career had brought him to London - but not just any part of London: Holloway Road. He was taken as a guest of the London show business agent Debi Allen, and it was the final home match of the season, but this memorable occasion, for an Irishman who has supported the team from afar for over 30 years, should have come sooner. Allen, who represents many industry luminaries, had met him at the Edinburgh Festival some four years earlier, and the two had hit it off. On discovering he was a fellow Gooner, Allen had offered to take him to Highbury whenever he could fly over to London. He had delightedly accepted and the two exchanged numbers, but then he did not hear from the generous agent again.

A few years later he met Allen and asked why she had not followed up on her offer. A bemused Allen explained that on more than one occasion she had phoned and left a message for him with a female who had answered the phone on the number he had given her. It seemed that Dara's then-girlfriend had not taken kindly to a woman from London calling to ask her boyfriend to fly over to go out to a football match and had decided not to pass the messages on. She was not his girlfriend for long after that!

So, despite the fact that his 'ex' had denied him the opportunity earlier, O'Briain finally accompanied Debi Allen to the 'Home of Football' to see both Pires and Jermaine Pennant score three a-piece in the dress rehearsal for the FA Cup Final a few days later. He recalls an entertaining game with an outrageous lob by Pires with an odd atmosphere as Arsenal had messed up in the league a few weeks earlier.

"After the match we went to that hut, the shack, the wooden lean to they called the Arsenal Supporters Club on the corner of St Thomas Road. We blagged our way in and they were clearing out the last of the supplies of whatever shitty beer they had got in for that season. So despite my misgivings Debi and I proceeded to drink the place dry."

His only other visit to the old ground was a 2-0 win over Celta Vigo in the Champions League, which set up the quarter final with Chelsea that was to end in disappointment. By this time, he was living in a flat on the Holloway Road, which may easily explain his love for the Emirates. Due to work commitments, even when offered tickets for Highbury, he was often unable to accept, but he was to be one of the lucky 22,000 who benefited from the move to a larger home.

Living where he did he would often hear the roars coming from the old ground, which made his inability to get tickets doubly frustrating. However, with the roars from Highbury echoing around the flats in which he lived, he could also see the new stadium progress and rise up.

O'Briain still looks back at his time in Holloway Road with huge affection, and with the Emirates being closer to Holloway than the old home, his affinity is with Arsenal's new home. Having watched every stage of its construction from his bedroom window he feels bonded to it. Holloway, for this ex-resident, just has so much character and is full of characters. It is the place where you can get anything you need at any time of day.

"PJ O'Rourke once said about Afghanistan that it is where the trade routes cross so if you wait long enough you can get anything you need. More recently in the book 'Gomorrah', about the Italian mafia, it was said the port of Napoli is where everything passes through. Holloway Road I think therefore belongs in the Port Of Napoli or on the trade routes of Afghanistan."

It is a few hundred metres from the finest stadium in the Premier League, and a place where you can buy gold trophies from a shop that only sells gold trophies, any amount of S&M gear from a row of specialist shops, and in between, you can pick up a second hand black cab or visit a department store called Selby's that is only there and nowhere else in the world. Not only that but for many years when he was not quite so instantly recognisable it was also the home to O'Briain's favourite Irish lock-in pub The Quays.

He recalls one of his earliest visits to the Quays was on an Easter Saturday, having made the long trek back from a gig in Galway on the Good Friday. He explains that in Ireland, for some bizarre Catholic hangover of a reason, you can only drink on a train or in a theatre on Good Friday. Galway is a university town and he could hear lawlessness out on the streets with the young people frustrated at everything being closed, whilst he was able to get slowly pissed after his show within the locked theatre.

"The next day, back in Holloway, feeling a bit the worse for wear, I went over the road from my flat to the Quays Pub. I walked in and the barman said, 'Hi Dara, my mother was the barwoman in the theatre yesterday and she says you had a good night' with a wink!"

From then on the pub became his lock-in for a time. The barman was on speed dial to have a pint standing in the early hours after a gig any time until about three in the morning. It was a proper Irish boozer, a place to watch football and chat. It was part of O'Briain's Holloway at the time, his love of Arsenal from afar transformed to feeling part of the Arsenal community. Sadly the Irish owner sold the Quays to a chain in the spring of 2016.

THE EMIRATES, NEW FRIENDS AND THE COMPLETION OF THE ARSENAL EDUCATION

Having watched new Arsenal emerge out of the Ashburton Grove site in the summer of 2006, O'Briain was asking around and sending out feelers for more regular ticket access. A bloke offered him a season ticket for the £900 value plus an extra £250 over and above. On closer enquiry it transpired it was the chap's own ticket and it was a loan for the 2006/07 season. The conversation thereafter was curt.

"'So it's not even going to be my ticket, it's a loan so what the fuck are you charging me 250 quid for? Funding your own ticket you chancer?' I basically told the guy to go fuck himself and he sneeringly said, 'Suit yourself mate. Why don't you ring the club and ask for one in Club Level?' So I said 'I will!'"

The truth of the matter was that he was not even sure what Club Level was, but he rang up Arsenal to enquire if indeed there was any availability. In what can only be described as a twist of fate resulting from O'Briain daring himself into doing something, Arsenal informed him that there was one season ticket that had just become available as someone had changed their mind. He had just been offered the last season ticket in the Emirates because he happened to pick up the phone that day. He nervously conferred with his wife who encouraged him to go for it.

"So I took it, but I was so worried because I was on my own and would not know anyone I would be sat with. I was not used to going to football, was anxious and thought this could be the loneliest thing in the world. Of course it is not and I could not have been more wrong."

Now ten years on, he has a group of close friends all from where he sits at the Emirates who are the most random collection of individuals. From London's premier Russian art dealer, to an early retired director of one of the major merchants, to the head of the Rain Forest Café, one of the largest restaurants in the city, to a guy who runs a successful photo agency.

"There is nothing that unifies us but we are like this Omerta group of people who constantly text and have been sucked into each other's lives. We jump all over each other when we score, we have been to births and marriages, thankfully no deaths so far, but to each other's phases of life in the last ten years. We go to each other's houses; we know each other's families and they are my Arsenal family."

So now to bring it back to where we began, with an eight year-

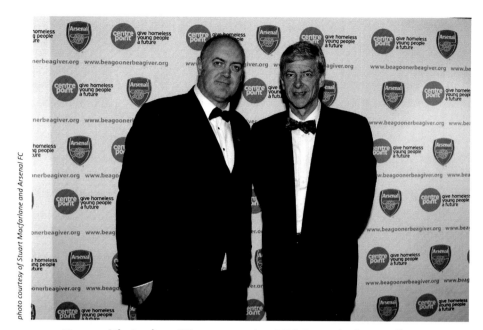

Dara with Arsène Wenger at the AFC Foundation Ball 2014

old Dublin schoolboy beginning his football education that was interrupted by hurling. Being able to watch Arsenal regularly from within the Emirates enabled the graduation to be completed; the square to be squared.

"Being in the stadium, watching the whole game, rather than just what the television chose to show on the highlights, was the real start of the football education for me. For years I had seen my football on this square, always drawn to the goal mouth action, and suddenly in 2006 I am seeing things in full view. Now all that talk about formations makes sense. I now get the overlapping; I get the two banks of four, I see what between the lines is and so on."

So you now grasp running the channels?

"No I still don't know where the channels are and quite frankly I am very happy to die not knowing where the channels are!"

He still believes for the Emirates to be truly Arsenal's home, the side need to lift a trophy on the pitch there. For him, however, not having the sentimental attachment to Highbury that so many have, whilst he completely understands how that is for them, the new stadium is his Arsenal.

"I get excited every time I go past the stadium and even more so as I approach it. It rises up in a part of town that I have lived and know very well like a 'mothership' that has landed."

Having said that he also accepts that the truly great matches and moments that have genuinely taken the roof off the place, can still be counted on two hands, which is something he regrets. He recalls the Henry header from an Eboue cross to beat United 2-1, after Fabregas had robbed Scholes of the ball. The Arshavin winner against Barcelona, 2015/16's last minute header from Welbeck against Leicester, the brace of 5-2 wins over the old enemy, one with the added sprinkle of Adebayor's dismissal, and not forgetting Henry's comeback at home to Leeds (but more of that later). It was as happy as he has ever been at football and Tweeted so, which did not go down well in Ireland!

A FUNNY THING HAPPENED AT THE CLUB

Since being a regular at the club, O'Briain had been very fortunate to have been asked by Arsenal and indeed some of their players, to be involved in an event or two. He knows he is in a fortunate position and is delighted to give something back and support the club when he can.

Hosting the auction at the AFC Foundation Ball in 2014 was one such occasion, and it gave rise to a personal favourite anecdote. The charity that year was *Centre Point* and the auction was to raise cash for that fabulous organisation in support of the capital's homeless. It did not take him too long to realise that the guests in black tie and cocktail dresses that evening were perhaps not necessarily those who frequented the Emirates regularly. Having been advised of the auction prize list he had prepared a few jokes he felt appropriate for a Gooner crowd. One of the prizes to bid for was a goalkeeping lesson with Wojciech Szczesny and O'Briain introduced this item with relish:

"He will teach you how to catch, how to block but mainly how to kick the ball against and an on rushing striker so it bounces high up in the air and scares the shit out of 60,000 people."

Suffice to say that Arsenal's then number one roared with laughter and no one else did. Undaunted, he continued on to the prize that offered the lucky bidder a chance to play on the pitch at the Emirates. For a while the leading bid was from the third choice Arsenal keeper Emilio Martinez who, at that point, had actually only played once on that pitch for the first team. O'Briain suggested the fact that he had 'never' played on the pitch was the reason he was bidding and once more the rehearsed humour found favour with the players, particularly the British ones, who got the jokes, but seemed lost on the paying guests.

Dara and Liam Brady catching up at the 2014 AFC Foundation Ball

The overseas players seemed entirely baffled at what they were expected to do on the night but one benefit of a photo with a bewildered looking Lukas Podolski, was that he got a follow from the German international on Twitter. He was able to send Podolski a direct message congratulating him on winning the World Cup and was rewarded with a reply: 'Thank you very much hahaha!' (Probably the message he showed Romesh on the set of *Mock the Week*.)

On another occasion he had met Liam Brady on the pitch when both were having their photos taken for different articles for the match day programme. Initially nervous, it was soon obvious that both worked for RTE on occasion and both were famous chaps from Dublin and the great man was an admirer of O'Briain's work.

"Sometime later we are coming out of a European match, me and all the lads who I now count as my close friends, and I felt a little kidney punch. I turned round and it was a smiling Liam Brady. So we exchanged pleasantries, had a little chat and I waved him off. I turned to my friends and sort of said sorry lads I was just chatting to my friend Liam there for a second and they were all looking daggers at me: 'Could you fucking introduce us to Liam Brady next time?'"

He explains that Arsenal had asked him to do an interview as a celebrity fan, to add some colour and variety for the programme. The photo at the head of this chapter was taken in January 2008, when he was given a tour of the ground and interviewed about his support, and for which he told a few jokes. The feature was then trailed on Arsenal TV along the lines of 'In the programme this week we have an interview with comedian and top Gunner, Dara O'Briain'.

At that time he had bumped into countryman Damien Duff, who was then playing for Newcastle, who Arsenal had beaten twice at home in the space of four days – once in the Premier League and once in the FA Cup. Duff told him that he had seen him recently. O'Briain, taken by surprise, had asked him where?

"He said, 'I was in the dressing room at the Emirates. I was sitting there looking up at the TV and there was a feature about you and a big picture of your face on the advert for the programme.' He said he thought to himself, 'I am really glad you are doing well Dara, but why the fuck do we have Arsenal Television on in the away dressing room when you have just beaten us three-nothing?' I did think he had a point. With a club that pays so much attention to detail you would think we would have the courtesy to turn off the home team promos in the away dressing room!" He says this last part with a wink and a grin.

He was also 'honoured', at the time at least, to be followed on Twitter by the then Arsenal skipper Robin van Persie who he had met earlier. After the Dutchman left Arsenal under a heavy cloud, the abuse he was getting saw him wind down his online account. O'Briain thought he would retain the connection whilst deliberating on one devastating parting shot, which the traitor would have to read. In happier times he is embarrassed to admit to quite lame direct messages to the then Arsenal hero.

"So I held on to the link thinking, at some point, I could pick the right moment and choose my 140 characters, as was still the limit then, and make them count. I could use this medium to play this trump card, write an intelligent version of 'Fuck you for leaving you whore. Apart from that, hope you are well?'"

The moment has now passed and the anger subsided, although perhaps a quick "How are the beaches in Turkey this time of year?" is still a possibility.

In happier times with RVP, Cesc Fabregas and Thomas Vermaelen, O'Briain has been asked by the three friends to do a turn at a charity event they had organised with their wives/partners to buy, as he recalls, some pitches somewhere in Africa. James Corden was the host and he had turned up to tell a few jokes. Again, he had written material especially for the occasion and one joke he described as very specific to the time at Arsenal, although he does suggest that you may not think much has changed. Thierry Henry was at the front table and he focussed on the Frenchman as he delivered his pièce de résistance to open his routine: *"In honour of the Arsenal team I want you to get the same experience watching me as I get watching the Arsenal. So for the first half I am going to be really really good, but in the second half, I am just going to be barely clinging on and it's going to be really scary to watch, okay?"*

As he delivered his line, all the punters laughed but Henry threw his hands half up in the air and gave him a look that said, *"I can't believe you have just said that."*

"There was a favourite moment early in my career when I actually got a man to spit out his beer and the Henry arms up in the air, as if to say 'Whoa sister', sits proudly with that memory."

HENRY, THE LEEDS GOAL AND THE BEGINNING OF THE WATCH SAGA

It seems fitting that we conclude O'Briain's story with his football education now complete, by returning to the Thierry Henry comeback goal – not least because it was the occasion that presented him with a new problem that as yet his scientific and mathematical brain has yet to fathom. He was initially struck with how all the players seemed primed to play their part in a wider scheme that night.

"What I was very impressed with was that all the players slowed down, so the whole thing happened in slow motion. The very kind Leeds players, with a fitting sense of occasion slowed down too, because you could see it from the first moment as he looked back to Alex Song and pointed where he wanted the ball rolled into him to score the perfect Henry goal."

As the ball nestled in the far right hand corner of the net Dara recalls that momentary dream-like state that sometimes comes when Arsenal score. It is as if all the sugar drains out of you for that split second and you feel euphoric, but faint, just before you all go completely bonkers!

"It was at that point I discovered for the first time that I had a very nice watch with a clip on it that only opens when we score a goal. Look as I shake my hand madly now, I can't recreate the motion that makes

it unclip itself, but every time we score and I celebrate, it loosens itself."

At this point it seems appropriate to mention the obvious: "Well, you are the scientist, Dara!"

"I know, but only the exact velocity of movement caused by my goal reaction makes it occur. It is like testing a seat belt in a car. You pull it quickly and it does not work and you can never quite get the same result as if you hit a wall. This watch is the same; I cannot make it happen by trying, but when we score a goal it flies off!"

With a watch that disappears off his wrist when we score it is perhaps a good thing that he sits in the posh seats with his group who have become his good friends in the past 10 years. Here's to hoping that the watch is flying through the air with increased regularity and he gets to see his team lift the Premier League title in his Holloway home-from-home. Let's also hope that when this happens he is there in his seat, which can be empty when he is on tour, and if he is you will not be able to read the personalised wording on his seat: "Dara O'Briain not on tour."

THE LAST CHAPTER OR SHALL WE CALL IT 'THE LAST LEG'?

I wanted to finish my journey into the world of Arsenal supporting comedy with the man who, in part, was my inspiration for this book. No, actually, he sits next to me at the Emirates and calling him an inspiration will go to his head. Shall we just say the laughs we have at every home game, both in the stadium and in the pub, gave me the idea. The truth is though, that Alex Brooker is an inspiration to thousands of disabled individuals in the country, showing them that anything is possible. I know this because he told me!

Joking aside, being born with shortened arms, hand disabilities and one foot without a bone, which meant that the leg had to be amputated at the age of 13 months, would be a challenge for most. But Alex is now flying the flag for the disabled on mainstream television. Brooker represents one of four legs between the three presenters of the *Last Leg*. A show born in the London Olympic year to cover the Paralympics, that has evolved into a show watched my millions covering all current affairs in a unique way.

IS THIS TOO MUCH ARSENAL FOR AN AUTOBIOGRAPHY?

It is a far cry from a journalism degree gained at John Moore's University and his role as a jobbing football writer covering matches that could not be further from his beloved Arsenal. However, there is an appropriate way to start Brooker's Arsenal story, and it is oddly with an autobiography that is planned but has yet to be written. He was excited to be approached by a publisher in the autumn of 2015 and asked to tell his life's story. Writing, as we will discover, was Brooker's first love. With conversations at an advanced stage, publisher and writer failed to see eye to eye on how to tell the Brooker tale. One issue was just how much of his story revolved around his love of The Gunners.

"The talks fell apart over a time issue in the end rather than the Arsenal one, but let's just say that one day, if I'm planning a book, it would be all about the Arsenal more than work."

So, whilst the book is sure to be written and deserves to be one day, at this stage the wider audience's loss is our gain as we get to enjoy the Arsenal stories that thread through Brooker's 32 years. Some of them may be coming to a television screen near you in the future, but that is a different story!

Ironically, the first Arsenal memory is both negative and linked to a negative life event. Despite being born in to the hard-core Palace heart land of Croydon, Brooker's father, whilst he was a huge football fan, never nailed his colours to the Palace or Arsenal mast. The first recollection of Arsenal entering his life was more of an unwanted intrusion for a nine year old with no interest in the beautiful game.

"I remember when my mum and dad had just split up and it was my ninth birthday. We (Alex and his two younger brothers) were visiting my dad at his flat. It was May 1993 and he had Arsenal v Sheffield Wednesday on, the FA Cup Final. I remember watching it with him and going home to my mum and she was like, "how was your day with your dad then?", I went, "he made me just sit there and watch football mum and it was so boring!"

His mum consequently had a huge argument with his dad, telling him that on the days he had his sons he should be taking them out and doing lovely things, not forcing them to sit indoors watching boring football. Of course, she was not wrong as it happens, as the first game of the 1993 FA Cup Final was an exceedingly dull affair – but that is not the point! Looking back and smiling at the memory his dad may have inadvertently sown a seed and subsequently his mum met his step-dad who was a massive Arsenal fan.

Within a year, after spending more and more time with a best friend at school who was a Gunner, and in his house, where football was always on, a young Brooker was turning. With his friends, Brooker played football more and more – both at school and in the park. So

Alex Brooker makes himself at home at the Emirates

much so, that the disinterest at being forced to watch an Arsenal Wembley final in May, was flipped on its head by Christmas. The irony!

"I ended up getting the video of both the Arsenal Sheffield Wednesday games for Christmas that year, along with my first Arsenal shirt and I went mad on it."

"I went from not being interested to the stage where you know when you are a kid there is only one thing you are interested in and it's all you care about. I remember watching the 1994 Cup Winners Cup Final with my dad and I was properly hooked all in a year."

He was soon surprised to find himself in the school (admittedly B) team, but not as surprised with the realisation that he was right footed!

"I found out that I was right footed even though I don't have a right foot, one of life's great mysteries. How can you be right footed when you have never had a right foot, well, not since 13 months old?"

The suggestion that it must be to do with the brain sending signals to the leg was met with...

"Yes well my brain has a wicked sense of humour and is having a laugh at my expense then. I have one normal foot so why not make that one my football foot, particularly since I am left handed as well?"

TERRIBLE TEENS

The first trip to see his now beloved Arsenal in the flesh came courtesy of a school friend and his mum, with whom he went to see a Champion's League match at Wembley in 1999. There was a slight problem though, in that teenage short-sighted Brooker forgot his glasses and, being high up and miles from the pitch, could barely see the players. His mate Leon's mum lent him her glasses but they hardly helped. *"I was so bad I was getting Overmars confused with Kanu! It was ridiculous and, so as you can imagine, I am not likely to forget my first time seeing Arsenal live, wearing my mate's mum's big thick glasses."*

His first Highbury match was in the final throes of the same season, in May 2000 and the visitors were Chelsea. This one was a bit of a blur for different reasons. A week prior to his 16th birthday Brooker had been through a rite of passage the night before. Yes it had been his first illegal under age foray into the pub. A night not easily forgotten for many, but as Alex recalls, it did not all go to plan. His friend Paul, who was 16 and had a fake ID saying he was a card carrying diabetic, had done this sort of thing before and, on arrival at the chosen 'Boozer', had issued his debutant pal clear instructions: *'whatever you do, don't attract attention to yourself because you look the youngest. Go and wait in the toilet until we have got the beers and we'll give you the all clear.'* Mission accomplished, and Alex was summoned from the urinals and handed his first pub pint, which of course he instantly dropped, beer and smashed glass everywhere, with the whole pub turning and looking at them. Paul: *'What did I say?!!!''*

"So anyway, at my first game at Highbury as a Junior Gunner in the Family Enclosure with my mates, I was suffering with my first hangover. I felt so shit, we won though."

At this time he was playing a lot of football for Disabled teams, even running out for Chelsea, but he admits he was overweight and putting considerable strain on his knees and ankle joint. Looking back, he played on much longer than he should have. He was playing or training and not able to walk without pain for up to a week afterwards. His love of the game overrode common sense in truth and it brought further operations, two above the knee and one on his ankle just so he could carry on. It was after one of the knee ops at Great Ormond Street that he was able to unexpectedly meet his heroes:

Whilst undergoing rehab after an operation, his physiotherapist had told him that the Arsenal team stayed at the Holiday Inn around the corner from the hospital before Champions League matches. She suggested that if he worked hard she would take him down in his wheelchair to see the players as they came out to board the coach.

"Because I was in a wheelchair, which I had to be because I could not use crutches, I figured they would know I was from the hospital, but as there were some other young fans waiting as well, I thought I am going to go for it."

As soon as he arrived inside the foyer, there was Arsene Wenger and, before his mum could catch him, a very forward 15-year-old, chubby Alex Brooker had introduced himself to the great man who was happy to chat, asking the young man why he was in a wheelchair. Alex, his mum and his step-dad had their photo taken with Wenger, and proceeded to meet most of the squad. Sadly, the snaps were taken on a disposable camera which his brother subsequently destroyed.

"I met David Seaman and Tony Adams, which was just after his book had come out. I told him how amazing it was. Strangely at that time my favourite player was Silvinho, and in the end, when we were waiting outside by the bus, every one of them came over to say hello, including the Brazilian. All of them, apart from Dennis Bergkamp who walked straight past me! I never felt quite the same about him since sadly, which is a real shame, as he was the first name I ever had on a shirt."

"It was embarrassing and funny in hindsight when Patrick Vieira came over and gave me a hug, because my step dad was a bit of a moron and said, 'Oh look Alex that's nice Kanu's come to see you!' He was just so nervous he got it wrong, he was just a plonker, there was nothing racist in it. It was one of the most embarrassing moments of my young life but Vieira thought it was hilarious."

Knowing Alex now, it seems odd to think of him as 14 and a half stone and in a wheelchair. But, as he explained, he had piled on the pounds whilst not being able to play football or do any exercise. For some reason though, I cannot shake the image of an overweight Brooker being hugged by Paddy Vieira, waiting for the coach to leave and then jumping out of the wheelchair and running around punching the air having met his heroes. Oh no, sorry – that would be Andy from *Little Britain*.

Part of the problem, obvious in hindsight and highly amusing, was that with the right lower limb and foot being false, he had never felt the fear of tackling as it was never him that would get hurt. Of course, this reckless approach had put additional strain on the actual limbs above the prosthetic, but he was not thinking that at the time.

"I remember crunching this fella so badly – I looked down at him and gave him the look, as if to say 'get up you wimp'. Walking off, I thought 'hold on, the foot feels a bit loose' and I thought maybe my studs had come out or something. But when I checked, the foot of my limb was pointing out left. I had hit the guy so hard I had sheered the bolts out where the foot joined the ankle of my prosthetic. My coach at the time, Nick, basically said 'Alex we've used all our subs you need to stay on'. I was like 'I can't', but he twisted the foot round straight and the gaffer taped it up so it was stuck together in one place, and I played the last five or ten minutes left-footed."

Should we be surprised that Alex played football with his disabilities? Honestly, probably not, as he was brought up to try everything, and to embrace all activities and sports. He does admit that cricket was an issue when it came to catching, although the unusual thumb and combined finger combo gave him an unfair advantage on release as a spin bowler apparently.

He never expected, or asked, for special treatment at school, and it was not until University that, for the first time, Alex was truly conscious of the disability and it was the football that brought it on. He was playing in a five-a-side league with mates every Sunday. But he would ache for days and days afterwards and would get so down and depressed at the situation. The anguish would lead to dark thoughts *"I mean, I was 21, could I not just play football for an hour on a Sunday and not feel so bad – surely that was not too much to ask?"*

"It bothered me for years and years. Oh God (Alex is crying). *"Sorry I did not expect to get so emotional, I have never told that to anyone before."*

Ironically, the decision to give up playing the game seemed to cause transference of emotion because the love for Arsenal replaced it. Most guys his age who loved football were still playing and going but Alex just began to live his football life through the Gunners. One of the by-products of this was that his emotions connected to the team escalated such that a win gave enhanced elation and a loss left him inconsolable for days – the exit to Chelsea in the Champions League quarter final in 2004, and the defeat in the Final in Paris in 2006, being cases in point. More of that later, but let's rewind to why Brooker was in Liverpool studying Journalism in the first place, because this path was also set in motion by, and linked to, the Arsenal.

JOURNALISM AND JOURNALISTS

Alex knew he wanted to be a football journalist from the opening year of senior school when he wrote his first match report for an English class. It was in September 1995 and his detailed write up was on the Cup Winners Cup Final Arsenal had lost to Real Zaragoza.

"Weirdly enough, most kids at that age have no idea what they want to be when they grow up, but I knew I wanted to be a journalist from the age of ten. I wanted to be a footy journalist and to be paid to write about football. Believe it or not, I realised quite early I wasn't going to make it as a player and made my peace with that. So I aimed for the next best thing. I thought I was good at English, I loved football and I knew a lot about it, so I wanted to do that."

From then on his desire to follow that career path never wavered. He could not give a jot about science or maths but just worked hard at English. Even at John Moore's doing a journalism degree, he paid scant attention to modules that weren't sports or football related. *"For example I scraped a pass around 40% in a Politics module but attained 97% in the Sport Journalism module. In my final year I was working at the Liverpool Echo as a Junior Sports reporter writing pieces like 'Eight Year old Judo Sensation,' but I made this the subject of my final project and was able to use all the reports I had written for the paper".*

He ended up in Liverpool as it was a top course and a great sporting city. Well, that and the fact that his A/S level results had not been great so his predicted final A level grades precluded him aiming for a few of the top colleges. *"I was doing work experience at a Kent Newspaper and I had to go to my school as a reporter to cover the A/S Results day and this wannabe writer got an E in English. That's not very good is it?'"*

He improved from an E to a B by resitting and for the first time in his school career asking for help. No one at the school had ever picked up on the fact that his disability made him a very slow writer so, for the re-takes of the A level exams, he received extra time and was allowed to use a laptop. It worked, and Liverpool and the degree in journalism beckoned.

"I went back to my school to do an inspirational talk, you know, as the boy who had done well. I thought I would try and be funny so I said 'yeah I scraped by here and never got bullied but I think that was because there were loads of gingers and kids more disabled than me.' And there was a lad in the front row in a wheelchair and I just had not seen him. The most misjudged joke I have ever told."

As previously mentioned, Alex was highly fortunate in getting an internship at the Liverpool Echo in the third year of his degree, which opened a few doors and much insight, but sadly sowed the seeds for early disillusionment with the only career he had ever wanted for himself. A high was being at the paper and working late on the night that the 'Robbie Fowler returning to Liverpool' story broke. There was just Alex and one senior Echo reporter left, and they got to break the story with Alex getting a couple of sidebar stories.

Only six days earlier he had been in the press box at Goodison for the visit of the Arsenal, shadowing the Echo Everton reporter, Dominic King, now at the Mail. He was walking up the stairs from the toilet and Arsene Wenger passed him. Even though, as we know, Alex had met him before, he was still so chuffed that he had seen him and nodded hello. He rushed into the press box exclaiming *'I have just seen Arsene Wenger!'* really excited, as you would be as a 21-year-old, wet behind the ears, student seeing the manager of your team. *"Only for some old hack reporter to turn round and with heavy sarcasm say – 'funny that, being as we are at Everton v Arsenal!' I suddenly thought 'all you lot are pricks, and I am preparing to go into an industry full of pricks.'"*

He had a similar experience at the Champions League Final. The Liverpool Echo had managed to get him a press pass. *"All they said to me was 'make sure you behave'. I was in the press box, everyone else had laptops, and I had been on it all day."* When Campbell scored, Brooker could not help himself and he jumped up and, in his own words, *'went ballistic!'* At that point a journalist from the *Express* told him to sit down and proceeded to complain about him, then attempt to get him thrown out. Alex had the valid press accreditation which saved him, but he has had an issue with national football journalists since.

As previously mentioned, Brooker had stopped playing the game he loved at this point and his passion for Arsenal had intensified. The depression after losses was awful, and the defeat in Paris left him very low, but events leading up to the match still make him laugh today. He and his girlfriend at the time had been saving to go on a dream holiday to Florida. But when he was told by the paper about a week before the game that he could go, he went to book the flights which, not surprisingly so close to the match, were very expensive. He had to pay £500 for a return to Paris from Liverpool.

The scene that evening played out something like this:

Alex's ex-girlfriend arrived home.

Alex: *"I am going to the Champions league final."*

Ex: *"Oh my God I am so happy for you, that's the best news ever!"*

Alex: *"There is a slight down side to it though love."*

Ex: An expression of realisation as it dawned on her; *"How did you afford to pay for the flight as I assume the Echo isn't paying?"*

Alex: *"Yeah I have used all the Florida money."* Gulp!

Ex: *"Get out!"*

Closing scene: Alex Brooker walks off down the road with a huge grin on his face.

"At the time I just could not care less as I was going to the Champions League Final."

After graduating, Brooker got a job at the Press Association where he stayed for six increasingly disillusioned and unhappy years, until the big break on the *Last Leg* for the London Paralympics. His contempt for the football journalist grew and, in his mind, now the majority of football journalists have a problem because no one trusts them or respects them anymore. *"In the Twitter age fans can see bullshit a mile off. We used to have to do a column at the Press Association called 'Football Confidential' and basically what we had to do was make it up. It was just based on a thought process, so for example Arsenal needed a defensive midfielder so we think Wanyama and the headline becomes 'Arsenal linked with £15 milion Wanyama.'"*

He does however respect the work ethic of journalists when it comes to match reporting and there is considerable dedication required. It is one of the reasons he fell out of love with journalism. When he got the job at the Press Association, he thought it would be amazing and a stepping stone to a position at a National paper. *"The reality sets in when you are travelling to Doncaster on a Tuesday night to watch them play Scunthorpe and you think 'this is not what I signed up for.'"*

It did not help that he had no interest in any other sport, so did not cover anything else. He only covered two games live in six years at the Press Association when his colleagues were doing two a week. He simply didn't want to do anything if it wasn't Premier League, so he ended up just being a website editor. He took other writers' stories and uploaded them on to the ITV Sports website. That was his job for the last two years. In short, the reality was not the dream he had from that young age, and it was only really Arsenal he wanted to write about. So, disillusioned, he was thinking of becoming a teacher when the opportunity came up at Channel 4 for the Paralympics.

I don't miss being a football journalist and most of them are just tossers! I have seen more arrogance in a press box at football matches than in four years working in television. Like Neil Ashton thinks he has the right and it's ok to say Ozil is stealing a living, but when van Gaal accuses them of being a little bit disrespectful, they get all hurt and offended. There is a real arrogance that I found distasteful."

The only journos he follows on Twitter now are the guys at the FA, Tony Barrett at the *Times*, who was good to him as a trainee at the *Liverpool Echo*, Dominic King at the *Mail*, plus Amy Lawrence and John Cross, purely because of their Arsenal connection.

NEGATIVE GOONER

So why does Brooker think he is such a glass half empty sort of an Arsenal guy?

"I mean I am a negative fan, you know that sitting next to me. I tend to think the worst these days and hope to be pleasantly surprised rather than be the other way. I used to have a more positive outlook, but I changed after that Chelsea game in 2004."

He recalls vividly that, having drawn at their place, we had the away goal and when we went one up at home with the Reyes goal, he thought the deal was sealed. In his mind we were at that point, the best team in Europe... or certainly the best left in the competition. Alex recalls turning to his mates and saying *"I can't wait for the Champions League Final, we're going to win this!"* We all know what happened next and Alex took it very badly. That disappointment was compounded by the Champions League Final defeat in 2006, and changed him into a gloomy Gooner.

"I was so convinced after Thierry scored the wonder goal at Madrid, and the way we dominated Juventus, it was to be our year, only again to be so bitterly disappointed."

When he and his now wife Lyndsey got engaged years later in New York, he was reminded just how much the loss in Paris had scarred him. *"We were waiting at the gate to fly home and, I don't know if you remember, but Arsenal had just bought out that Henry film and I was watching it on my iPad. It was a one hour documentary and he talks about the chance he had when he went clean through on goal and it would have been 2-0 and game over. I had never heard him talk about it before and he said that he had run all game and it got to that final moment of destiny and he did not have any power left in his legs. So there, at the departure gate in New York, I just started bawling my eyes out. Lyndsey was like 'what are you doing Alex there are lots of people*

looking at you?' I was so upset and everyone must have been thinking that guy is having an emotional breakdown."

In 2015 he got to meet his hero, Henry, at the Sky Sports Studios, which was incredible. He has met and interviewed many high profile celebrities, but to meet Thierry he describes as one of the best moments of his life. Or perhaps, on reflection, it should have been;

"I only had a few minutes with him in the Sky Sports Studios and, as I had my photo taken with him, I blurted out, "I had a cardboard cut-out of you at my wedding and you are my hero. So I had the opportunity to say anything to my all-time hero and I said that!"

Okay, so it does sound like he came across like a star-struck teenager, and that he did better in 2000 when he was only 15 and in a wheelchair meeting the team, but what on earth did he mean by the cardboard cut-out comment?

What he had wanted, or meant, to say would have been quite cool – that every table at his wedding reception was named for an Arsenal player. A friend of Alex's is an artist, so each table had a cardboard cut-out of a replica kit on it with the player's name and number on the back [pictured above]. So, for example, there was a Liam Brady table with the old 70s kit, a Charlie George table with the yellow Cup Final

'71 kit, but Alex and Lyndsey's top table had a larger Thierry Henry one in the sliding knee celebration.

"So that is what I wanted to explain to him, but it came out all wrong. I still have them and I really want to put them up in the house. I wish I had not said it the way I did as he probably thinks I am a complete saddo, but it was still amazing to meet him. And he smelled just like I thought he would smell. He smelled like success, like someone who should have a statue outside the ground."

FEELING PART OF THE ARSENAL

A decade after hanging up his boots, Brooker is now playing again. So what has changed?

He explains that, as he was quite overweight as a kid that did not help with the extra strain on his joints. But years later, as an adult, he has lost loads of weight and it seems to have changed things. In making a documentary about his *Perfect Body* for C4 in 2012, he did a huge amount of impact training in the gym. This programme had him enduring far more impact than he had as a teenage footballer. Unlike back then, however, he found he was not getting the resultant debilitation and pain. It was this pleasant realisation that caused Alex to resurrect his 'career'. Initially he was 'rusty as hell' but he is progressing. So is the once left footed player still right footed?

"Yes, even though the coach has said I can't shoot for shit and he wants me to use my left. I try and angle my body but, ultimately, it could go anywhere and there is no predicting what I will do. The only good thing about having the prosthetic leg is that it is in a fixed position so perfect for side foot passing. So I am going to try that more for shooting. Long balls are not as much of an issue as it is seven-a-side."

So with one nightmare over, after a decade without kicking a ball, another boyhood dream has been fulfilled. Because the above coach, who trains him and his team mates every other Tuesday, is his Arsenal coach, and as we speak, his first game for the Arsenal Amputees team is coming up - away at Pompey in the FA Amputees League.

"I probably would have played even if I still did find it painful to be honest. I couldn't turn down the chance to play for The Arsenal!"

Indeed the success that has come to this affable young man has been a pleasant surprise to Brooker, but he has undoubtedly made the most of it. Not only by diversifying his work and experience on television and not taking it for granted, but by working extremely hard for several charities he believes in. The other aspect that the success has ushered in is the ability to feel more part of the club he loves.

He recalls watching *Fever Pitch* and the main character feeling detached from Arsenal living in the suburbs and wanting to live near Highbury.

"That's why I wanted to move to Highbury and, for the two years we spent living in an overpriced flat in the old Highbury and getting a season ticket, I kind of felt more in tune."

Brooker and his wife have now moved, but after the FA Cup Final parade on May 31st is a particular memory about living in the old Highbury that will long remain.

"I didn't do myself any favours on Cup Final Parade day. I came back and she (Lyndsey) was sunbathing in our shared garden, which of course was the old Highbury pitch. I was like this is all so amazing, I collapsed and I started bawling my eyes out again with the emotion of it all. She had to take me in I was so drunk, but I was just enjoying the fact that I was laying in the middle of the pitch at Highbury and we had just won the FA Cup again."

FAVOURITE MATCHES

His favourite all-time game that he was at was against Juventus in the Champions League in 2006. He recalls that our ex-skipper, Vieira, had come back and at that time Juventus were a really good side but Cesc absolutely bossed it. *"The noise, I don't think I have ever heard noise like it at Highbury. It was so loud on the night and almost deafening at times. To be fair it was like that all the way through our run to the final. I just loved that game though for the atmosphere."*

For the great night when Arsenal won the title at Anfield on the 26th May 1989 he was only five and he has no first-hand memories but his step-dad had a tape of the full 90 minutes.

"I have watched it so many times over the years. It's like as a young fan when you chose your team you want to educate yourself about the history and traditions of your club so I watched the season review as well. I would have given anything to have been an adult fan like I am now and watched that live. That is up there with my favourite Arsenal games."

In terms of away games, the Old Trafford away FA Cup Quarter Final victory over United he rates as the best ever, but also City away when the Gunners won a few months earlier in 2014/15. He vividly remembers it for the display and the result but also a rather stupid City supporter. It was a breakthrough performance against a rival, a great atmosphere and particularly so as Brooker, with the Arsenal away fans, found himself very close to the City fans.

"One of these was right next to me and he kept counting his fingers in front of me. I was in the Arsenal end but we were quite close to them. I thought to myself if someone said to me right now you can have the digits or the 2 goals which do you choose I would have taken the goals and I simply could not understand what he was thinking. Whether he thought he would get to me and I would think 'Oh I better not celebrate that fact we are beating you on your own patch cos I have only one thumb and no fingers!"

IT'S ALL ABOUT THE ARSENAL

There is an excellent chance we will see an Alex Brooker scripted sitcom based closely on his student days, so you may just have had an insight into one or two of the funny Arsenal related episodes that may appear. However, I hope it is fairly obvious that for Alex and his life, past present and future it is quite a lot of 'all about the Arsenal'!

"The truth is that all of the moments in my life, the core ones at least, I link to The Arsenal. If someone said to me what were you doing when you were 11? Well it was the path that led me to my career in football journalism I refer back to Arsenal v Zaragoza and my English lesson match report. When I was in hospital I think of meeting the Arsenal players and Wenger. All the periods or moments link to football so I can't do the biography without it. My nostalgia is Arsenal, even as I said my parent's divorce I attach to an Arsenal related memory. It was probably quite a sad time but I have attached the memory of a boring Arsenal game to it."

Not forgetting getting married with a cardboard cut out of Thierry!

ACKNOWLEDGEMENTS

I do hope you have enjoyed the end product of a hugely rewarding journey for this particular Arsenal fan. Obviously for a book like this there are many people I would like to thank. Each and every comedian who contributed, gave freely of their time and for that and their personal stories, given with such candour, they each have my gratitude. In particular though, I would like to thank Alex Brooker, my friend and the initial inspiration behind this project and Ian Stone for encouraging so many of his peers to get involved.

Thanks to the team at Comic Relief for their appropriate endorsement of this book and I do hope the contribution you receive as a result will be significant.

A big shout out to those at Arsenal FC who have supported me with advice, promotion and in particular photos – Stuart Macfarlane, David Price, Andy Exley and Mark Gonnella.

I would add my appreciation to Boyd Hilton for his wonderful foreword, Lucy Grattan for her proof reading, the very talented Jamie Fulker for his superb cover artwork and needless to say Dave Lane at Legends Publishing.

Lastly to all my friends my family, particularly my wonderful wife Jo for putting up with me juggling the project and the day job.

FOR MORE INFORMATION ON OUR
COMEDY GOONER CONTRIBUTORS

Ian Stone http://www.ianstonecomedian.co.uk
Chris Martin http://www.chrismartincomedy.co.uk
Marks and Gran http://www.marksandgran.com
Gary Marshall http://www.garymarshallcomedian.co.uk
Romesh Ranganathan http://www.romeshranganathan.co.uk
Carl Donnelly http://www.carldonnelly.co.uk
Tom Rosenthal http://www.tomrosenthal.net
Jim Campbell http://www.thefootballramble.com
Dara O'Briain http://www.daraobriain.com

FOR MORE INFORMATION ON COMIC RELIEF

http://www.comicrelief.com

ABOUT THE AUTHOR

Dave Seager began writing for fun as a regular guest on an Arsenal site in the summer of 2011. By 2012 he had launched his own blog for his Arsenal related musings and in 2013 he bought into *gunnerstown.com*, which along with his friend Paul Hepker, he has grown to be seen as one of the larger Gunner portals. Dave still writes regularly for *gunnerstown* as well as being the Arsenal columnist for the *football.london* website.

In 2013, he was approached by the family of Arsenal Football Club legend, Geordie Armstrong, who wanted a fan to produce a book in memory of one of the club's greatest servants. In partnership with Legends Publishing, *Geordie Armstrong on the Wing* became Seager's first book in the autumn of 2014. His conversational style, engaging with umpteen interviewees who were keen to share their memories of Armstrong, received critical acclaim.

Two years later, Seager has employed the same style to inspire and cajole an incredible number of celebrity fans from the world of comedy to share their Arsenal stories. The result is a thoroughly original and amusing romp, full of humour, banter and never-before-shared stories from some of the UK's favourite funny men.

Geordie Armstrong on the Wing **is available
online from www.legendspublishing.net**